UNDERSTANDING LIBBY

A MOTHER'S JOURNEY WITH CHILDHOOD PARANOID SCHIZOPHRENIA

CHARITY MARIE

DEDICATION

This book is dedicated to Liberty and Phoenix, who give me the inspiration to write each day. This is also dedicated to Robert, who supports my crazy need to write. Lastly, to Skip, who has been a father to me for more than two decades. I am proud to be a part of your lives and thank you for changing my life for the better every single day. Everything I am and will be is thanks to your love and support.

This book is also dedicated to all the struggling parents who are uncertain and desperately seeking answers to the mental health crises and situations in their life. May you find answers and peace throughout your journey.

UNDERSTANDING LIBBY

FOREWORD

THE END OF 2017 BROUGHT OUR FAMILY TO A CRISIS point on all fronts: emotionally, financially, mentally, and spiritually. Our family, once with a strong bond of unity, was fracturing and splintering in numerous ways I never could have foreseen. Nothing in my life could have prepared me for what we were facing. 2017 brought me to my knees in ways I never imagined were possible. It brought fears we never experienced before, and a look at a future that terrified us to the core.

But, despite all that, 2017 also saw us making incremental progress forward. One crucial element was created: understanding. We began, for the very first time, to truly understand what we were facing. We began to find some answers amidst all the fear and uncertainty. You cannot move forward without a good understanding of where you've been and what the problem is. As we learned all we could about schizophrenia and its symptoms, we began to unravel the puzzle of mental illness affecting our child and our family. We found ourselves fighting for information, empathy, and strength at every turn.

2018 will see us start the year with a series of new medical crises, and an almost immediate hospitalization to start the year. There are moments of joy, of intense pain, of sacrifice, and new solutions. It will see us reach new highs and new lows as we continue to battle toward answers and solutions to Libby's symptoms. Sometimes, it has to get worse before it can get better.

.

PART TWO:

NAVIGATING THE MAZE

January 2, 2018

ANOTHER BUBBLE BURSTS

Today was another day with a surprise at the end. At 8 p.m. Libby began having chest pain, shortness of breath, severe pain all over, and hot/cold flashes. Initially, I figured these were just a side effect of her meds. Then, she stopped breathing and responding to me. Her eyes didn't blink. For about ten of my breaths, time stood still.

I had the horrible thought that I'd somehow lost her – that she'd died right in front of me. It was so surreal I still feel like I must have imagined it. It must have been a dream. And then suddenly she breathed, and she looked at me. She immediately registered the panic on my face but couldn't understand why. "What's wrong Mommy?" I couldn't find the words to tell her. I just called 911.

The paramedics took one look at her and barely asked if I wanted to transport her. It was obvious – she was ghostly pale, in a lot of pain, and almost catatonic. In the ER they did the same things they always do, except for this time, the supervising doctor made a startling announcement: "Are you aware she has a heart murmur?" For the second time today, I felt my breath catch in my chest. The world began to spin impossibly fast, and I became very dizzy. I was sure I was going to faint right in front of this doctor.

After a moment, I recovered my ability to speak and began babbling questions. How is this possible? How could it have been missed? Libby was just here on 12/26 and no one said anything. She's been healthy. Is it the medication? I had talked with the nurses on 12/26 about her strange heart rates with higher and lower fluctuations, and they had assured me it was fine. In typical ER fashion, he had no answers other than that I should follow up with her pediatrician.

Now Libby sleeps, looking so small in the hospital bed and so peaceful. And I can't process it all – the pain, the fear, the horror. This just can't be real. I want this to be a dream that I will wake up from. What are the chances this will be an "innocent" heart murmur when she's already lost consciousness once, even though briefly? Is it caused by the medication? Was this issue lying in wait all this time, ready to spring on us? My side of the family has a long history of heart issues, but I figured they had skipped Libby, as they had skipped me. Now I'm glued to the heart monitor, watching it, and internally cringing every time it drops and starts to beep its alarm of warning. At one point her beats per minute dropped to 56 from 72. The doctor is guessing she may have a prolonged QT syndrome. This was a resource I used to learn more.

http://www.heart.org/HEARTORG/Conditions/Arrhythmia/About
Arrhythmia/Types-of-Arrhythmia-in-
Children_UCM_302023_Article.jsp.Wks0xt-nGM8

A few minutes ago, Libby said a series of things that broke my heart even further.

L: "Am I going to die?"

Me: No, we're not going to let that happen. That's why we're here."

L: Good.

A little while later...

L: "I'm glad to be your daughter."

Me: "That's good. So am I. What made you say that?"

L: "Because you love me."

That I do. More than life itself. More than I ever could have imagined. The last ten years have been hard but beautiful. Libby has taught me unconditional love in a way I never thought possible. She's inspired me to be better, to grow and learn in ways I never would have without her. She has helped to heal me. I cannot imagine life without her in it. Even now, with the schizophrenia and this, I wouldn't trade a moment of being her mother. I regret any time I was ever less than grateful for her.

January 4, 2018

A LONG DAY

I'm very tired right now. I'm not exactly sure why. Today was a good day overall and I got a lot done. I even managed at the end of it to make sure the puppy pen got cleaned by my son and scheduled a psychiatrist appointment for Monday afternoon for myself. All I can say is thank goodness for virtual visits. For $30 I can talk with a psychiatrist on MY schedule.

Quite honestly it was the only chance I had in making it happen. I don't look forward to trying to explain to the psychiatrist that I'm depressed and anxious because my child is mentally ill and that's never going to change. There will be good days and bad days, and a constant strain of stress. I'm a pretty high-strung individual to begin with, but when one combines this kind of stress, well, it's a good recipe for disaster. Hopefully, this doctor will understand and be one that's willing to prescribe long-term medication.

I guess I'm just too tired to blog now. Libby is stable again, the heart issue that scared us so badly a few days ago seems to have gone away now that the Lexapro is gone. That situation was far more dangerous than I would have liked. I hate to think what would have happened if I continued to have her take that medication. It very well could have led to the death of my child, which is an exhausting thought.

January 5, 2018

CLINGING TO HOPE

It is hard to believe that it's been already been three weeks since Libby came home. It seems impossible that things have changed so drastically in such a short period. I feel like I've lived and aged multiple years since then. One year for every week, maybe? I barely recognize myself internally. What we've gone through these three weeks is a bit beyond description, like how fast we've been forced to learn and adapt. Much of this has been instinctual, and a complete reaction to the various crises that have occurred. In a way, such drastic change was necessary and could only be brought about by deeper understanding.

I've been having a lot of conversations with people on the schizophrenia.com forums and one thing I have recognized is common with us all is a refusal to give up. We might fall, we might even lay there for a bit, but as parents, as family members, we get back up, dust ourselves off and keep going. Day after day, week after week, year after impossible year, we get back up. Some of us lose the battle, and the ones we've sworn to love and protect. The battle was still fought every day until that point.

A part of me is afraid to look too hard at the possibilities of the future. What I would consider there would prove my unraveling. I talked with my husband, and he wants me to accept a bleaker reality than I can do. I have a penchant for believing a thing is possible well past the time another person would have given up. There's an indomitable, stubborn, persistent, refusing-to-give-up part of me that just keeps doing, no matter what. It's hard-wired into my DNA.

I told Robert I can't give up hope. If I do that, I'm dead. This illness will win. Hope is what keeps me going, hope that together we can beat this somehow. I never want to stop fighting until we win.

January 6, 2018

EXHAUSTION

Yesterday started as a completely normal day. Things seemed to be going well. I was working from home, and Libby had a therapy appointment in the morning. We went to the therapy appointment and then to lunch at a favorite restaurant. By the time we were done, she began to feel dizzy and was stumbling a little bit. We got in the car and the ride home became a nightmare I couldn't imagine. At one point I had to pull over, because she thought she was going to vomit. Pulling over on a 75MPH highway is nerve-wracking, but so is watching your daughter heave and spit. At that point, I was contemplating the ER. Then she lost consciousness. Twice. It was like someone flipped a light switch. At that point, the ER became a certainty, so I drove her myself.

We spent seven hours in the ER while the medical staff monitored Libby. They also triggered her panic and paranoia disorders by trying to force an IV. We eventually were able to get her to comply with some anxiety meds, numerous coping techniques, and a little brute force. They eventually admitted her to a room for observation and further testing. They monitored her through the night, and I was able to get a few hours' sleep. The doctor did tell me that in addition to a urinary tract infection, she also has gastroenteritis, which is inflammation of the stomach lining.

Just a little bit ago, one of the doctors came in to talk to me and tried to convince me that the cause of her loss of consciousness was due to the stomach bug. I was instantly enraged. A stomach bug doesn't cause loss of consciousness. It just doesn't. They didn't say it, but it began to feel like they just didn't believe me, although I can't be sure if that was my own internal feelings. Everyone was professional, but I was hearing a lot of "we don't know" responses, which was really aggravating.

Maybe I haven't communicated the symptoms appropriately. I've been looking online for resources to help explain this. The definition of unconsciousness as stated by WebMD is:

Unconsciousness is when a person suddenly becomes unable to respond to stimuli and appears to be asleep. A person may be unconscious for a few seconds -- as in fainting -- or for longer periods of time.

What are signs that a person may become unconscious?
- *sudden inability to respond*
- *slurred speech*
- *a rapid heartbeat*
- *confusion*
- *dizziness or lightheadedness*

These signs are exactly what I saw happening with her on multiple occasions.

There's a list of possible reasons:
- *low blood sugar*
- *low blood pressure*
- *syncope, or the loss of consciousness due to lack of blood flow to the brain*
- *neurologic syncope, or the loss of consciousness caused by a seizure, stroke, or transient ischemic attack (TIA)*
- *dehydration*
- *problems with the heart's rhythm*
- *straining*
- *Hyperventilating*

We can rule some of this out just through common sense and process of elimination. Libby's blood sugar wasn't low yesterday as we'd just finished lunch. Both prior times she experienced lost consciousness, she'd eaten food not long before, and she's been eating very well lately. We found she was mildly dehydrated in the hospital, but it was not significant at all. She wasn't straining or hyperventilating at the time. So that leaves syncope, low blood pressure, seizure, or problems with heart rhythm.

They've hooked her up to a heart monitor several times, including all last night, and had the results reviewed by a cardiologist who said there's no issue, but we'll get further evaluation on Monday. They are hooking her up to an electroencephalogram (EEG) now and will monitor her brain waves overnight.

The doctors have evaluated her medication and ruled it out as contributing at this point, to the best they are able. Anything is possible, but from what I understand the chances of medication being the cause are slim, and as close to not likely as we're going to get.

At this point, I don't know if I want there to be a result or if I don't. On the one hand, having my fears confirmed in some way would be a relief. At this point, any confirmation would also be very serious, and we really don't need another issue. The doctors have assured me the "heart murmur" is very mild, so much so a less experienced doctor wouldn't even hear it, and "innocent."

The strangest part of this is *I* am directing her care. If the doctors had their way, they'd just release Libby as fine. That's what they tried to do this morning. They don't have to deal with this at home. They don't have to watch her not respond. They don't have to be terrified every time it happens. They don't have to wonder if she will come out of it. Honestly, they don't probably even care if she doesn't survive it, but I care. I care very much. Even though I'm more exhausted than I've ever been in my entire life. There's just no end in sight at times.

I'm so far out of my depth with all of this. It's so complicated trying to figure out whether the meds are causing the issues, or whether it's something else.

Using logic again, Libby's been physically healthy up until recently. She's never had a major medical issue. The only real physical change was medication. She's never lost consciousness before. Hopefully now they'll monitor her brain, she'll get her

Risperdal dosage tonight, and maybe they'll monitor her while she sleeps. Maybe that will give us some answers.

I'm praying for both answers and for there to be no issues. Is that crazy or what? If there are no findings, it will be an extremely costly checkup. If there are findings, our future will change once again, possibly in a slightly worse direction. And all I can do right now is wait.

January 7, 2018

HUNTING DESPERATELY FOR ANSWERS

We got discharged late this morning. The hospital has no answers other than Libby's lab work is normal, as is her EEG and her ECG. We have a referral to a new psychiatrist, are establishing with a new PCP, and have a cardiologist appointment tomorrow. The hospital couldn't tell us much of anything. Isn't that amazing? In this day and age, they have no answers in the inpatient setting. It really makes you wonder what the hell hospitals are for. We couldn't see the psychiatrist, because it's a weekend and not an "emergency". Yeah, maybe not for them, but we're hunting desperately for answers.

Libby woke up very off this morning and we're unclear as to why. Her memory is off significantly – so much so she didn't know what day it was. I'm exhausted and trying to recover my strength after the severe stress and trauma of the last few days. Everyone is in their rooms, including Libby, who is taking a nap.

WHY DO WE FIGHT?

I mean, I get it. We're different people. Robert copes his way; I cope my way. I try to be tolerant and understanding. I try to give him space to process and cope in whatever way works for him. We're both humans, so we make mistakes. Tempers flare. It seems to me like he picks fights deliberately when things are at their worst for me. He makes me feel attacked, on edge, and like I have to defend myself from him. He says these awful, hurtful things that I can't help but react to. He knows what things will push my buttons, and instead of shutting up, he deliberately attacks me with them. I grit my teeth and try to keep my mouth shut until I can't.

A perfect example: Phoenix fell tonight. He slipped in the hallway on the wet tile. We think he's likely fine; he's just going to be sore tomorrow. Hubby and I decided to go out for ice cream as a break, and he asked me about an appointment Phoenix had with a chiropractor. I had to cancel it because I was in the ER at the time with Libby. In the grand scheme of things, it wasn't a priority. A lot of things have gotten shuffled around in the last few days, including me cancelling real estate showings with a potential client (he doesn't know about that, there wasn't time to tell him nor was there any point). I let him know I canceled it on Friday.

At this point, Robert proceeds to tell me I need to take Phoenix to the appointment tomorrow. Oh really, so you're my dictator now, telling me what to do? He didn't ask me, didn't suggest it, he just told me I'd need to do it. At which point I snapped and said, "I do have to get some work done tomorrow." I'd already missed much of Friday and Tuesday of last week. I have client work I haven't been able to do at all. I already have two doctors' appointments that day scheduled and will be missing work anyway.

This little situation became a full-blown fight. It was our first time together semi-alone in over a week, and we're fighting. Robert tried to give some bullshit apology, and then proceeds to say some other jerk off thing, "you've been focused on Libby for two weeks and now Phoenix is hurt and could use some attention."

As if I've been neglecting or somehow ignoring our son who was just hurt within the last hour! As though I'm doing something wrong for being focused on helping Libby. When Phoenix had breathing trouble early last year, I dropped everything, juggled everything, and turned over every stone to try to help him. I was focused on him for months, but when I do it for our other child, who is in a worse crisis and has a much more serious situation, somehow, I'm doing something wrong? What the hell is that? We had three ER trips with Phoenix for breathing trouble, and I don't know how many specialists' visits. I handled these by myself, while hubby was on the road. I juggled my schedule, made the sacrifices, and did the work while Robert sat back and did his job.

I'm a single parent every day while Robert is on the road. The burden and responsibility for both kids is on me 24/7/365. I don't even really get a break when he's here. What the hell is the point of being in a relationship if you're never IN a relationship? Why am I staying in this relationship? What the hell is the point? I'm not saying what he does doesn't help and isn't necessary, but for crying out loud - don't be an ass to the person who's handling the lion's share of the work here.

I just spent the last almost 72 hours in a hospital room with Libby - terrified, uncertain, and trying to figure out what's wrong with her. I've barely slept. For her sake, I had to shove down every single emotion and reaction, hold my tears at bay so I wouldn't upset her. I was home for less than five minutes and dissolved into tears. I'm still not done processing any of the last 72 hours. The fact that we have no answers doesn't help. I'm completely shot in every possible way – physically, mentally, and emotionally. My spirit is as low as it can possibly go. The minute I get home Robert is telling me all these things that we need to get done. I don't give a shit about any of that! Who cares about selling puppies when my child is hurting, and I have no idea why; when I don't know when or where she'll collapse next?

The sad part is, tomorrow I probably would have taken Phoenix to the urgent care to get checked out. Maybe at lunch or right after lunch. That thought had already entered my head, but I wanted to give it 24 hours to see how he felt first. He wasn't screaming and wailing in pain, he just hurts. Even when I was trying to evaluate Phoenix, Robert kept trying to shut me up. I'm the one who's here for these kids every day. I'm the one who sees them through every medical crisis and have for the last three years.

After work, I'd get Phoenix examined and get him some kind of pain meds, maybe a shot for pain. I just hadn't gotten there yet because I was too damn tired! I wasn't ready for yet another crisis on top of the last 72 hours. I'd just spent the last 24 hours thinking Libby could have a seizure disorder. For crying out loud, let me decompress a bit first.

I have seriously got to get on some medication. I cannot cope with any of this on my own. I'm so overwhelmed by it all I can barely think, and I'm so tired I can't sleep. My insomnia has gotten so bad I've taken to waking about every 20 minutes or so. Even two Benadryl did nothing but let me sleep for an hour or two.

I really hope tomorrow is a better day. I don't know how much more of this I can honestly take.

January 11, 2018

FIGHTING THE GOOD FIGHT

On Monday I got some medication to help me with managing some of my emotions. and So far after four days it seems to be making a difference. I am at least able to be more effective at work and am doing a little better than just managing the critical stuff. Of course, it's only been four days, so we'll see.

It's so hard to believe it's been four days since I posted last. Libby is back inpatient at the behavioral health hospital. We lasted 19 days. Of those 19 days, five additional days involved hospitals. I missed three unplanned days from work. I am hopeful this time gives her what she needs to succeed. She had a pretty good day today, or so the nurses say. Maybe the hospital is just the kind of environment that keeps these things at bay. She's had good days at home and school too though, so it doesn't mean a whole lot.

I'm still fighting every day. Fighting for Libby, for her mental health, fighting to try and keep our family together even as we fracture and splinter under the pressure. Never in my life did I imagine I would be dealing with something like this and I have learned very quickly just how little of life I understand.

I didn't understand that every day could be a battle just to wake up, or that it could feel so abysmally hopeless and pointless. That's what it's like for Libby. How she's still sane at this point is beyond my imagination. She had six hallucinations yesterday, and by the end of it she was sobbing and clinging to me, begging me to make it stop. She was happy to go to the hospital, in the hopes that it would make the hallucinations stop. Now I'm left, once again, to try and put together a plan for her return. I have no resources to do that. I'm working to plan for my meeting with her psychiatrist on 1/16 in the hopes that will help.

My little fundraiser isn't doing very well, and I'm not sure what that means. I'm not sure if I'm just not "advertising" right, if my message is wrong, or if it's just the wrong time of year and people are broke. If everyone donated the price of a cup of coffee it would add up fast, it doesn't even take much. At this point, I'm not sure what I'm going to do to pay her bills – any of them.

January 18, 2018

OLFACTORY & GUSTATORY HALLUCINATIONS AND RESIDENTIAL TREATMENT

Libby just completed her third inpatient stay at the acute center. Less than 24 hours later she's already had a visual hallucination and an olfactory hallucination. We uncovered that she has those tonight when she told me the rice crispies tasted like rotten eggs. Investigating further, we discovered that this isn't the first time she's experienced that, and that other times food had tasted "rotten" or "poisoned".

At this point, we have no choice but to find a residential program for Libby to help with some of this. Doing anything less for her is just subjecting her to it all over again, and a slow devolving into crisis is inevitable. I am absolutely determined to give her every tool, advantage, and help she could possibly need on this journey. I won't rest until I've done everything I can possibly do to help her.

The hardest part is the realization that even tastes have betrayed Libby. That is something that is so integral to life and joy that my heart and mind simply can't fathom it. I sit here munching on Lemon Heads (hey, it's one of my stress relievers) and wonder what it would be like if they suddenly didn't taste how I expected them to - what a betrayal that would be. Then to find that lots of foods are that way but not all the time seems too cruel.

I tried to help Libby tonight to understand this new symptom we've uncovered, and once again I feel like I'm walking a dangerous tightrope between giving her the information she needs, craves, and demands, and protecting her just a little longer from the awful truth. Libby is grieving too – every day – for the little girl she thought she was, for normalcy that she no longer has. She feels betrayed and wants someone to blame. I have tried to make sure she doesn't blame herself, and so far, that seems to be working. She's also promised me that no matter how much she wants to, she will not hurt herself. I have told her it's okay to think it and want to, but never to do so. I hope it's enough. I hope I have surrounded her with enough of my love and devotion to protect her. If I could put a protective talisman around her, I would. This is as close as I can get. Each day I work to add to it – showing and telling her every day how much she's loved, trying desperately to inject her with love.

January 23, 2018

OVERWHELMED & FALLING APART

I came down with a fever last night. My son was diagnosed with the flu type A, so now I have it too. I'm taking Tamiflu but still feel miserable physically. On top of that, Libby has steadily devolved once again to the point she wants to cut herself. Now, we're leaving in the morning to admit her into the acute center in San Antonio. Once she's stable enough they would transition her to the residential program. I'm such a mess I can't even blog about it. Maybe tomorrow.

January 24, 2018

HEARTBROKEN DOESN'T DESCRIBE IT

I admitted my ten-year-old daughter into a residential treatment facility for an unknown length of time today. It could be anywhere from 30 days to eight months or longer. I drove 2 1/2 hours to do so. What would drive a mother to do such a thing? That's what I would have asked three years ago. Now I know firsthand: desperation, fear, hope.

Our family is desperate for answers and solutions to the myriad unpredictable symptoms afflicting Libby. More than that, SHE is desperate for help. Even at 10, she realizes she needs help to fight this. If she's going to have any chance at all, it's going to take an army to equip her for the battles she will face for the rest of her life.

Fear has driven us to this point. Fear of watching Libby struggle and lose a little more of herself every day. Fear that one day she will lose herself completely and be unable to come back to us again. Fear that she will succumb to her desires to die.

Finally, there is hope. I hope that someone can help. I hope that somehow, against all the things I've read, and all that science understands, that Libby can be the exception. I hope that somewhere inside her, waiting to be unlocked, is a wealth of strength like what I have within me. I hope that we can find a way to open it, and that strength will be enough to see her through all that lies ahead. I hope, most of all, for the person Libby can become, if somehow, we can fight back this dreadful mental illness enough to let her thrive; if we can part the veil and let her achieve some of her potential. I cannot make myself give up hope that somehow, as impossible as it may be, that there can be a way for her to heal.

I am beyond shattered, beyond heartbroken, beyond devastated – I am lost, adrift, unmoored, terrified. If this doesn't work, I've got nothing left. The next step is permanent institutionalization. The next step is beyond horrible, beyond inconceivable. It may be beyond my strength. If I must give up my child for her own good, I may very well lose myself entirely. I'm holding on right now through sheer will and determination, and for Libby's sake, but if I must watch her slowly lose her complete grip on reality, I may follow right behind her. I already feel like half of my spirit is gone. The grief is raw and consuming, and I can't find a way to break free.

I can't adequately describe how this feels emotionally. I would rather be tortured in a million ways or die than have her endure this. I would not hesitate to take this for her. I would give anything to save her from this, to spare her. My soul screams, "Why her?!" What possible purpose can this serve? If everything happens for a reason, what's the reason for this?! There isn't any! This is just cruel, horrible genetics and biology. My instincts told me I should not have a child and I did it anyway. Was I tempting fate? Is this the cost: to witness her unraveling, to witness her death?

I want to find a purpose for all the pain, anger, fear, despair, fury, and grief. I want to kick and scream and rip the world apart at the seams. I want to move heaven and hell. I want answers. I want redemption. I curse God. I pray to Him for help. I am every emotion at once, yet empty at the same time. I smile and laugh at the same time I cry. Inside I can't stop screaming.

Be the change you want to see in the world, right? I'm so angry, and I'm so overcome with grief I can't think.

January 25, 2018

REMEMBERING FIRSTS

I remember the first moment I realized I was going to be a mother. I was sitting in a bathroom, waiting for a pregnancy test to tell me what I already knew. After all, I'd already felt different for two weeks. I'd been voraciously hungry, and my breasts were constantly aching. I was eating sunflower seeds like crazy, something I never craved. My body was telling me everything I needed to know about the life growing inside of me.

The moment the pregnancy test changed to positive, I was still stunned. It was really happening. I was 26 years old; my career was fine. However, I wasn't exactly in a relationship I was sure about. In fact, I'd been planning to break it off. In that instant, a seismic shift happened inside me. This was no longer about me. My life was now about the tiny human already growing inside of me. For better or worse, planned or unexpected, Libby would be my responsibility for the remainder of my life. I already loved her.

Keeping her wasn't even anything I had to think about. Although her father had other ideas immediately, I squashed them in no uncertain terms.

It didn't take long before my emotions began to get the best of me. I would cry at sappy commercials or sad movies. It was like being pregnant was triggering some emotional awakening as my body changed. I cried at her ultrasound. Listening to Libby's heartbeat was a miracle I have no words for. That whooshing sound had me sobbing in an instant, partly from relief to hear how strong and sure it was.

I was doing things I would never do for myself – like getting a tetanus shot, a flu shot, monthly bloodwork, prenatal vitamins. Nothing but the best foods I could find. And I was constantly eating. I was driving my co-workers nuts with all my eating, but the cravings and the need for food were maddening. For such a small person, Libby sure was demanding! She seemed to love fruits, vegetables, and cereals, as that's what almost all my cravings were for. Meat made me nauseous, but I still forced myself to eat steaks, chicken, and whatever proteins I could.

As Libby got bigger, we played for hours. I would poke my belly and she would kick or try to grab my fingers. I listened to music at a high volume, so she could hear it too. At the same time, my relationship was falling apart and causing tremendous stress, as he gambled and would be out until the late hours. As my due date neared, we fought about everything from money to cleaning and everything in between. Friends helped me make sure I had everything I needed for Libby's arrival.

I remember the first time Libby looked at me. Her eyes seemed so clear, so alert. They seemed to say, "Oh, finally, there you are!" I fell in love. I couldn't stop looking into her perfect blue eyes. Every emotion was so unexpected. I was flooded with so much love for her that tears just poured down my cheeks, and I didn't care. I was happier than I ever thought possible. I didn't understand why I was her mother, but I knew I would do everything I could to be the best mother I could be. The first night I barely slept, just held her and occasionally dozed. She barely cried, because she'd open her eyes and I'd be right there to greet her. The nurses wanted to put her in the nursery, but I refused. She'd been with me 24/7 for nine months already, I wasn't about to separate from her now.

Breastfeeding for the first time was hard and took four nurses to help me. For some reason, Libby just couldn't seem to understand what she was supposed to do, and neither could I. By the time we were discharged, we were pros. The hospital was so pleasant overall, I didn't want to leave. It didn't help that my C-section was healing, so every step hurt. The doctor had cut me pretty much from hip to hip. The first step was the most excruciating pain I've ever experienced in my entire life. I still don't have anything to compare it to eleven years later.

The first day at home was so peaceful. I had no idea of what was going to come. All I could do was watch Libby sleep in her crib. It seemed so big and she seemed so small. I kept checking to make sure she was breathing. My heart just melted every time I looked at her. I don't know how much time I spent just standing there, marveling at her tiny perfection and feeling full to bursting with joy.

I remember the first time I left Libby at home with her father. I don't remember why, I just remember I left for a few hours and it was dark when I returned. When I stepped in the door, I instantly knew something was wrong. Libby was shrieking at the top of her lungs - not crying but shrieking. I rushed into the bedroom to see her swaddled in the middle of the bed, face beet red. Sitting inches in front of her was Shannon, her biological father, his back to her as he played furiously with a game controller, a video game at full volume.

In that instant, I felt a fury the likes of which I have never known. I rushed to Libby and picked her up. She immediately stopped crying and looked at me. Her crying resumed a moment later, but this time it was her more normal cry that she was hungry. I could smell she needed a diaper change as well.

Shannon paused his game and watched me as I immediately began to nurse her. I berated him in a quiet fury. He said she hadn't stopped crying since I left. His baffled look was more than I could take. I got her settled down, fed, and cleaned, with some diaper rash ointment for her irritated behind from being left in a dirty diaper for hours. Then I took him into the living room and laid down the law.

I told Shannon he could either be a part of Libby's life or he could leave. She was barely three weeks old and he'd rarely even held her in all that time. It was clear to me he didn't give a damn about her. If this was how he was going to be, he could leave and good riddance. But if he left, he had to stay out of our lives forever. I would seek child support and nothing else from him. At that point is when he decided to tell me he'd never loved me. This was fine with me, even though it hurt like hell. I let him know our relationship was over, he could sleep on the floor until he could find somewhere else to stay. It wasn't long before he was gone, living in a homeless shelter.

A friend of mine with four kids of her own, who were all in school during the day, would watch Libby for me so I could work. I didn't live very far away and would drop her off and pick her up each day. Life continued to change, and I struggled every day to build a better life for her. I fought to be a better person and went through therapy for almost two years to deal with my own demons, to avoid repeating past mistakes. That first year was hard, with so many firsts, but it was worth it. I would do it all over again. Loving Libby is worth it. Being her mother is worth it. Even with the heartache in our lives right now, I wouldn't trade being her mother for anything in the world. That's probably the biggest one of all. I've always put her first in everything I do. I always will.

February 3, 2018

PROMOTION

It's been almost a week since my last post, and some of that is because life has gotten a little calmer and a little less stressful. Having Libby in the treatment center has really been a life-saving situation. We're all slowly decompressing from the stress of the last six months. She's doing well currently, and today we spent the day together. We went to Subway, then to Ashley Furniture to pick out a new couch. After that, we visited the mall and then Walmart. It was a great day and a lot of fun considering how little we did.

Probably the highlight of the week, though, was getting promoted at work. I sat down with my supervisor on Friday and he offered me the official position of Office Manager for our office, as well as a promotion to Litigation Assistant.

I'm probably too exhausted right now to truly convey my enthusiasm for the future.

February 5, 2018

PEELING BACK THE ONION LAYERS

Today we had our first family meeting. Up until this point, it's just been me and the therapist talking about the issues, but today we dove into some of the issues as a family, and it was very illuminating. The therapist and I were able to identify a lot of issues with Libby's problem-solving skills and mental thought processes including fortune telling, catastrophizing, projecting, distorted reality, and distorted thinking. I don't have any idea how her thinking got so convoluted, but boy is it jumbled, even in the simplest ways.

Somehow, everything is fear based. Now if someone gets angry, Libby gets afraid. If I get angry, she internalizes that and believes it means I don't love her, or someone is going to hurt her. I can trace all this back to my ex-husband, Ryan even though she can't remember it. His verbal abuse of me and verbal and physical abuse of her has created some crazy layers we're trying to peel back. It's affected her ability to trust and feel safe, as well as her ability to reason properly.

The therapist has her work cut out for her. We were able to help Libby address a few current issues, and then tried to help her to see that people are human and sometimes get angry - but that doesn't mean they don't care or never will.

March 1, 2018

A HUGE DISAPPOINTMENT

Once again, our medical system has failed us. Libby was discharged from the residential treatment program yesterday after a month and four days of treatment. Not only was this without consulting me, it was with barely 24 hours' notice. At the time, they claimed insurance wouldn't authorize more treatment. I investigated it and found that to be false.

For whatever reason, they discharged Libby a week after adjusting her meds and in the process had me blaming the insurance company. The insurance company quickly set me straight, after I sent them a letter promising to hold them liable if anything happened to my child due to her release.

The psychiatrist failed to diagnose Libby prior to her discharge. All the scheduled testing wasn't even completed yet. Now we're in limbo land with just as many answers as we had to start with, which is zero. I'm baffled. How and why? How could they just stop treating her and why would they? The insurance company even stated she met the clinical criteria for more treatment.

My spirit and soul are so weary from all of this. I am weary of battling to get answers against a system determined not to give them. They just flat out refuse to do so. For the life of me, I cannot understand why. It goes against all logic and common sense. Through it all, my daughter suffers from the unknowing of it, the uncertainty. We're left struggling, yet again, to help Libby and unable to figure out how to do so.

Libby is still hallucinating frequently, and while I accept that will happen and medication can't necessarily stop them from happening, her fear and anxiety are hard to witness.

Thankfully, we were able to make some changes before Libby came home, including having my husband here to help her full time and to manage the house. Financially it's already very hard, but we'll make do somehow. I received word we'd be getting a grant to help, which would be wonderful whenever it comes.

I feel so defeated, lost, afraid for the future, and angry - really angry. I know this will pass, I will find a way as I always do, and things will get moving in the right direction again. It's a set back and while this battle may be lost, the war can still be won.

March 2, 2018

UNEXPECTED SUPPORT

I received two great phone calls yesterday from our insurance carrier, Blue Cross Blue Shield of Texas (BCBSTX). With all the negative publicity on insurance companies lately, I must give some praise to the team involved in Libby's care from the insurance side. It's not very often one can praise an insurance carrier, but her team responded immediately to my email.

Within 24 hours, they'd conducted a review and contacted me to let me know what had happened on their end. Documentation will follow. In the meantime, the staff member who was part of the review team called and left me a two-minute message of support. She expressed sorrow and compassion for what we're dealing with. Her message lifted my heart because someone, somewhere, recognized how much we're struggling and felt compassion for that situation. Some days, that means a lot. Yesterday was one of those days when it was really needed.

Being dropped by the facility so unexpectedly is a blow that has left us reeling and trying to understand. It feels like the bottom dropped out from under our treatment world. I have emailed the therapist to understand why. My husband is convinced someone screwed up and they'll never admit why. I'm less certain of that, but willing to consider it.

Libby does seem to be much improved over where she was a month ago. I'm just not certain that it's permanent. We've had so many times when the treatment has failed to allow her to turn a corner. I'm encouraged by the delight of her teachers who comment on how great she looks. She's almost bright and shiny for her, which is always what happens with a med change. And then the hallucinations increase, her anxiety increases, and we're right back where we started. But if this even gives us a month of peace, I'll take it. Being able to hug her every day is such an amazing blessing. It's an adjustment to having her home, and we're walking on eggshells, but being around her is so wonderful.

Libby is still having a lot of hallucinations, which creates anxiety. I'm not confident the medical providers fully understand her symptoms and are medicating the end result of the cycle, rather than the root cause. While it's effective for now, helping her to cope with the root cause of her symptoms is very important. Now we wait for puberty to hit, which will cause all of it to unravel again. We've been warned that while she's stable now, puberty will absolutely, undoubtedly change everything. If we're lucky, we'll have two more good years before it gets so much worse. The thing that gives me hope is that deep inside of her, at her core, she's a good girl and wants to be. I've seen it firsthand, and I am fighting for that little girl every single day.

March 2, 2018

A (MEDICAL) STONE WALL

We attempted to get a proper diagnosis for Liberty, and it appears a stone wall has been erected once again preventing us from getting the right diagnosis. Everyone has complete backtracked and that led to her discharge immediately. I cannot for the life of me understand this bullshit stance of refusing to diagnose someone with schizophrenia before they turn 18.

Libby was discharged two days ago from the residential treatment facility she was admitted to 36 days ago. We've been in a mental health crisis since July 2017 when we discovered she was hallucinating, and we've been living in a revolving crisis for much of the last two years. Her discharge was a surprise. It's taken me two days to understand what happened, because initially we were told insurance wouldn't authorize more care. The treatment team 100% blamed insurance for not authorizing more care. It wasn't just one person – it was the therapist, psychologist, and psychiatrist.

In a self-righteous advocate's fury, I emailed my Case Manager with BCBSTX that I would hold them legally liable if anything happened to my child because of their refusal to continue her care. I called the decision reckless and criminal. The Case Manager's response 12 hours later was baffling – BCBS had not only authorized her continued treatment, but she still met the clinical criteria for care. The Case Manager with BCBS was baffled that she'd been released.

Next, I thought someone dropped the ball. A mistake had been made; someone didn't communicate to the right person at the right time. I contacted the Utilization Management teams for both the facility and insurance, to find out what happened. As it turned out, both were aware of the approval of more treatment, had communicated the information, and it was a treatment team decision to release Libby.

If you're lost or scratching your head at this point, you're not alone. I reached out to the treatment team again only to be told, yes, the treatment team made the decision. This was done without consulting me, without even explaining it properly, lying to me the whole time. Did they think I wouldn't take action on it? They obviously don't know me very well if they thought for a moment I would just let that go. I FIGHT for my kids every single day.

If that means I have to tear the insurance company apart brick by figurative brick, I will do exactly that until I get what Libby deserves. That's not to say others don't, but I won't rest. My husband says I'm relentless in advocating for our kids, and it's something I'm good at. There's nothing that will trigger my self-righteous indignation more than feeling like things aren't fair for them.

I'm a passionate advocate for my children and would have raised holy hell on Libby's behalf to get her treatment. Now, the wind is out of my sails and I'm baffled. We went from a psychiatrist who was willing to properly diagnose her with schizophrenia to suddenly labeling her symptoms as trauma-based anxiety. WHAT?! Of course, she has trauma-based anxiety! Jesus, even I knew that! It's trauma-based anxiety because she sees things that aren't real and can't tell the difference! Are they subtly accusing me of my child being physically abused in some way? Is someone abusing my child and I don't know it? If she's being abused, I cannot tell it. She says no one is touching her inappropriately, no one is hurting her. Still I wonder, does Libby know something I don't? Is she hiding something from me? Did she disclose something to the team I don't know about? They legally must tell me if she's in danger, so it can't be that.

I have done extensive research on anxiety, I've read the studies, and I'm no dumb bunny. I may not know everything there is to know about medicine, but the basics are clear to me. Yes, anxiety can lead to mild hallucinations of a visual or auditory nature, but they are mild! They are not full-blown, terrifying visions of creatures from another world dripping blood from their fangs and claws.

Libby sees things that have no logical explanation at times when she's not even stressed! There are no identifiable triggers, it's completely random and surprises the hell out of her every time. Sitting in the car yesterday, she says a werewolf just appeared out of thin air on the seat beside her. Not there one moment and poof – there it was. This leads to anxiety and fear, even panic, which is logical and understandable.

If random realistic beasts appeared out of thin air near me, I'd be scared out of my mind - Anyone would be. Libby no longer runs away screaming. She has learned some ability to cope with it. The terror she lives with all day every day is enough to rip a hole in my soul some days. Still she fights it! Every day – with courage, and grit, and sweetness, she fights for sanity. She wants desperately to be "normal" and does everything she can to be that way, despite all her symptoms. It's so unfair.

I am so damn tired of doctors treating the results of the symptoms instead of the symptoms themselves. What is it going to take for me to get them to recognize this for what it really is? It doesn't fit in a nice neat little box. I get that. What do I have to do? Am I just dreaming to think I will ever get her diagnosed before 18, so I can protect her and take care of her? Is it just impossible? Am I fighting the wrong battle?

They will tell me they think it is schizophrenia, but she's too young to diagnose. What is that? Is there some law I don't know about? How can it possibly be ethical to misdiagnose or underdiagnose someone and give them treatment as a result? She is not getting the full benefits of proper treatment because they won't diagnose her properly. I can't get anywhere for her – No SSI, no Medicaid.

The financial burden of this is all on my husband and I – and it's horrendously expensive. $120 a week for Libby's therapy alone – $480 a month, and I have no idea where I will find that money. I make $33K a year and am supporting four people now that my husband is home full-time to take care of the kids. That's $6,200 a year, almost 19% of my income. Who can sustain that?

The only thing to come out of this is an emotional disturbance (ED) label for school, which will put Libby into a special education classification, but she already has that because of dyslexia. It might allow for a smaller class size in middle school, and more one on one help, but that may be it. She's already getting everything she can from the school system. She's been getting unwritten weekly counseling from the school counselor, so we'll formalize that. We'll have a formal Admission, Review and Dismissal (ARD) meeting in April or May to prepare for Libby's transition to middle school. This scares the crap out of me because if kids are tough in elementary school, they become vicious in middle school. She's automatically a target because she's different, so that will get worse.

Don't get me wrong – I'm grateful. I see improvements in Libby. I'm thrilled she's home. It's where we want her to be. Not, however, if she's still struggling so hard every single day. The problems are NOT solved, by any means. We don't know what we're supposed to do with her at home, or school, and things likely will get worse once again. Whether it's a month, or three, or six, it's almost guaranteed we will be back here again. That just infuriates me to no end. There's so much more that could and SHOULD be done for her. WHY are the people who are responsible for doing that, refusing to help her? She's trying, she's doing everything they tell her, she's putting in the effort. So am I. So is her father. So is the school. Why won't they help her further? Why did they just stop?

Why have we been battling for so long only to keep ending up in the same place? At this point, I need therapy from the stress of it all! Where's my advocate?!

March 4, 2018

NO PSYCHOSIS

For the first time in a long time, longer than I can really remember, Libby is not in an episode of psychosis. She doesn't walk around with a glazed look as much (although at times she does still space out) and she is communicating so much better than before. I was able to send what I hope is a nicely worded letter to her therapist, to wrap things up and make it known nicely that I was displeased with the way things ended for Libby. There's already been a lot of fallout from them just ending her care so unexpectedly. We were completely unprepared to catch her when they just dumped her out of the center.

In the end, no matter how much I may hate the situation, I can't change where we are now. All I can do is offer grace and forgiveness, along with the acceptance that some humans made mistakes. Libby will suffer for it, and I have made it known in the hopes it doesn't happen again. That's about the best I can do with the situation, and work my ass off to help her, as I've always done.

At least we have a therapist and a psychiatrist. Things aren't great at school, but we'll work through that on the fly. We're working to find a dog for her that can help with her anxiety and be a constant companion for her. With the right training, hopefully, it will help her with her anxiety. I'm not exactly sure where to start but have reached out to a couple of places in the hopes of finding some help and resources.

May 20, 2018

THE STORM IS BREWING

It's been a long time since my last post and that's likely not to change. I am busier than I've ever been before so finding time to blog is hard. If I'm not busy working, I'm too exhausted to think. I'm certainly too exhausted most days to feel. Of course, this is part of my own internal coping mechanism. It's not necessarily a good coping mechanism, but for the time being that's the only one that's working.

Libby's doing okay, although I worry for her physical wellbeing. The meds are effective, but there's a toll on her body. She gets stomach cramps really bad; the meds also lead to severe dehydration. Just one day without the meds though, and she starts exhibiting symptoms. It's a fine balancing act – keeping her sane and lucid versus her body needs. I can't imagine the effect these meds have on her internally and I know of other mothers who have lost their grown children to heart failure and other issues, potentially due to the medications. But what kind of life would she have without them? We can communicate with her now. She's emotionally more stable than I've ever seen her, and with less anxiety. Her hallucinations, as far as I know, are pretty much stopped.

We received notice Friday that Libby qualifies for Social Security Disability. I'm still not 100% with that. It's one thing to suspect, but to have a total stranger agree is an overwhelming, scary thing. I want so very much to be wrong. I want someone to tell me I'm crazy, that she's just a kid and she'll grow out of it. Why can't I just be wrong? Why did I ask questions that led us down this path?

My logical brain knows she can't outgrow this, but my heart wants so much for Libby to be a healthy, happy child. It doesn't help when people try to convince me she can have a "normal" life. I've seen her at her worst. There is no normal life with that. The meds are delaying the inevitable. This is as good as it will get. That's not me being depressed or pessimistic. It's me being realistic. Considering my track record for being right, it saddens me to see it as clearly as I do. I wish I could have ignorance.

My heart breaks every day. There's an impossible, overwhelming grief locked in an internal box that there's no time to process. It's full of all the broken dreams and hopes that happened last November. This is just one more thing to add to the box. This is one more thing that says my child will never have a normal life. She will struggle all her life. We will battle these internal demons and will likely lose. I can see the day when I will lose my child, despite fighting with every ounce of strength I possess. For the time being, the meds are working, until they no longer do, and then we start all over.

I've been working from 5:30am – 10pm every day. During the day is my Paralegal job and our source of income and insurance. At night, everything is about real estate. So far, I've got three sales in process, and two listings. I'm working with about 80 clients so far, and that is growing every day. Hubby is working to get licensed as well, so we can grow our little business. I'm working to build a team by the end of the year so that we can cap and keep 94% of our commission instead of 70%.

Finances have become extremely dire, so having those checks will help tremendously, I hope. In addition, we're waiting to be awarded food stamps, and I'm hopeful after addressing some paperwork, that Libby will get Medicaid. The costs for her therapy have sunk us rather quickly. It's a miracle we've lasted this long. We cashed out hubby's 401K and have used all of our savings, which was over $10K. We're trimming as much as we can, but at $30 per appointment, it adds up so fast. And of course, we're doing the same for our son as well, who has autism. All told, it's $120 a week for mental health for the kids, plus gas.

This month I haven't been able to make our car payment for the first time, and our utilities have been cut off three times. I haven't paid a single credit card bill. The water bill is late. Our cell phone bill is late. Our cash reserves are gone. Skyrocketing electricity rates haven't helped – we're stuck paying $.21 cents per kWh right now because we can't afford the deposit to change companies, which is $320.

I've reached a point when I just can't care anymore – I just put my head down, bust my ass day and night, and hope everything works out. I hope they don't repossess the car. I hope we don't get evicted. I hope every day I can make it work. I hope for relief and respite from the stress. I cherish every moment of peace. There's not much laughter in our lives right now, not much joy. We're just sitting and watching, waiting for Libby's symptoms to change. It's an impossibly hard thing to be stuck in this limbo while still trying to move forward.

We had a meeting at the school last week and Libby was given an emotional disturbance and special education status. She's got more accommodations; the school is are now aware of her issues. I blew the lid off confidentiality. I just don't care about it anymore; I'm so driven to protect her in the school system. The meeting was over two hours, as we worked to bring everyone up to speed. Afterward, I was wrung out like a mop.

I hate this. This illness has completely rewritten our lives; just completely turned it upside down and inside out. Even so, my true heartache comes from knowing every day for Libby is miserable, and that without the meds, she's internally driven to want to die. Part of me gets the desire, because a lot of times I feel that way too. If I were alone, with no one depending on me or needing me, I wouldn't hesitate to kill myself. Who would miss me? Who would even notice or give a damn? Even if they did, it certainly wouldn't last for long. My life is but a blink and while I'll have a ripple effect on others around me, my impact is nothing. A few years after my death, my name will have faded along with my memory. That's just how life works. I'm beloved and cherished by four people in this world. And honestly, that's enough for me. I don't need worldwide adoration. I have more now than I ever expected to have.

That's where we are, and that's all I have the energy or time for.

August 5, 2018

WORKING FOR THE FUTURE

After more than eight months of extremely hard work and determination, we've finally reached a level of stability I wasn't sure was possible. Having hubby at home managing children has really freed me up to focus and do what I'm good at, which is working. I wasn't raised by traditional parents and have not had role models that gave me the skills to be a parent. I'm honestly the last person who should have borne a child. It doesn't mean I don't love her with every breath I take, but I know Libby doesn't get everything from me she should. I'm not terribly affectionate (with anyone), or nurturing, or even sometimes very interested, but I give everything I'm capable of. Right now, that's working to build a future for our family. I received a much-needed raise in late May, and then have had 24K in sales, which has replenished our cash reserves and given me a little breathing room. We'll likely lose the SSI, but I'm okay with that. Libby will still maintain the disability status, even if she doesn't have the income. For the time being, that's enough.

I was able to replace the Toyota with a Kia Sorento, and we're just waiting for them to repossess the Toyota. It was just financially stupid to continue paying almost $500 a month on a vehicle with 175K miles on it. We'd paid $20K already on it, with $12K remaining. I'd tried to renegotiate something with the bank, or refinance it, and they refused. We made payments on time for over 3 years and it just didn't make sense anymore. We couldn't see paying it off, so we invested in something newer. It'll hit Robert's credit, but since he's not working it won't really matter. I'm working to fix my credit so we can get back on track to buy a house next year. I'm going to take a huge hit on taxes this year (I owe $6K so far), but my income will be close to $70K. All in all, real estate is saving us and hopefully will continue to do so. I'm grateful for every new transaction, every new prospect and opportunity in this business.

Libby seems to be doing okay. She got a horrible case of lice, so bad we had to shave her head just so we could effectively treat her hair. I'm combing lice and nits out daily. The best thing for her has been tea tree oil. The over the counter stuff doesn't work on her anymore, so that's been a huge headache. Phoenix got them too; so far I'm clear and so is hubby. Hopefully, it stays that way.

That's the latest. The summer has been quiet. We started Libby with a new therapist who specializes in paranoid schizophrenia and autism, in the hopes she can help Libby with better coping skills. The difficulties Libby has with understanding reality just blow my mind and are not anything I'm equipped to deal with. Robert started fiddling with her meds and reducing her anxiety meds, which immediately caused symptoms. He didn't understand that the anxiety meds are a combination drug for handling depression, help her to sleep properly, control her suicidal impulses, and her anxiety. I finally got him to dose her properly when she came in and told us both that she was depressed and suicidal again.

August 6, 2018

A SURPRISE CALL

I received a call while at work today. Someone reported us for medical neglect due to Libby's hallucinations. Within minutes I was in tears on the phone. I informed the lady at Child Protective Services that this was the third report on my child in two years. I described to her all the ways we've been working with, and struggling to help, our child: the therapy we couldn't afford but paid for anyway, the recent inpatient stay, and the fact that she hallucinates and there's only so much we can do to stop it. All we can do is manage her symptoms.

We scheduled an appointment for Wednesday evening. I told her to look up the prior history and that our door is always open for them to come anytime they like. We are doing nothing wrong and have nothing to hide from anyone. If someone has a better way for us to manage this terrible disorder, I'd love to hear about it. I could use all the help I can get!

August 7, 2018

CHILD PROTECTIVE SERVICES

CPS called today to let us know they would be closing the investigation, and to cancel our appointment for the next day. Their words were, "the allegations were unfounded and unmerited." My husband and I are both baffled. Libby had a sleepover on Saturday, to spend time with a friend who would be moving to Germany. We asked Libby if anything happened or if she had any issues. She said everything was fine and she didn't have any hallucinations.

I wonder if someone from the school could have reported her, but the staff all should know and understand her emotional disturbances.

I cannot understand why someone would do this. It feels cruel, malicious and uncalled for. It hurts my heart so much to be accused of neglecting my child in anyway. Libby is my whole world, and I love her with every ounce of my being. If I'm doing something wrong or not doing something, it's because I don't know to do it and am just doing the best I can. I wish I could talk to the person who made the report and explain things.

August 9, 2018

A BIZARRE TWIST

In a bizarre twist, I received a call at work today from Libby's new therapist. She admitted to me she called CPS and reported us for medical neglect. I am astounded. Not just at the audacity, but the fact that she jumped to that conclusion after forty minutes, without even talking to me. My husband and I are both livid, to the point we will be writing a letter to the owner of the business, who is a friend of mine. At least we know now, what little good that does us.

The ridiculousness of it has me stunned. How can I trust therapists after this? This so-claimed expert accused me of coaching my daughter on her symptoms, because she was too educated about them for her age. Are you kidding me? I could not believe my ears. You'd think by now nothing would surprise me.

Then the self-doubts kicked in. Have I been coaching her? I thought back to our conversations. No, there was no coaching. I asked her to describe things she experienced but didn't put any words in her mouth for her. Her descriptions of things were very clear in many cases, allowing me to match them up to her symptoms.

Eventually we did help name them, so she would understand what was happening to her but only after verifying what she was experiencing. She understands a lot. She's a patient with mental illness, she should be educated on her illness. Why would you deliberately keep a child in the dark? This woman is just nuts.

September 17, 2018

RELAPSED

We made it six months, but the start of the school year and entry into middle school proved too much for Libby. Her internal defenses crumbled under the onslaught. And here we are trying to pick up the pieces all over again.

By the time she was admitted, Libby was a miniature raving lunatic – pacing, crying, growling, shredding tissues, kicking and punching and slapping the walls. Yet another wound to my soul was experiencing her at the edge of her self-control, barely able to control her rage over nothing any of us could see or experience. At one point she screamed at the voices only she could hear, "I will not hurt them, I will die first."

Apparently, the hallucination told Libby to hurt us, but she had just enough of herself left to fight the commanding voice within her. All the while, the staff acted like it was no big deal. I just wanted to shake them! Do something, stop her suffering! I get they are trained not to react, but it left me trying to manage the situation. Were they studying us or testing us, or did they not know what to do with us there?

It took a week and more than doubling Libby's antipsychotics to get her lucid again. She is back residential again and so happy. She finally recognizes it as a place of safety and a place where she can be herself without fear. So now we must start rebuilding her again.

One of the big flaws has been the outpatient care. Libby's outpatient team doesn't care about her, isn't invested in helping her, and half the time doesn't believe anything she or we say. All of this is beyond frustrating. I just want people to help her. The people who should care about her, have the tools I lack, and understand what's happening to her won't do anything. My own helplessness is like an albatross around me mentally and physically. There is no greater hell than being helpless with what your child needs.

I have been trying to develop my own coping skills for the situation, with Robert's help. My mantra has become "control what you can, and then let the rest go." I can't fix Libby. I can't fix the situation, and it's not my job to save her. This is her journey and as much as I wish her journey to be easier, I can only witness it, walk with her, and support her as best as I can. I can put every resource I have into this but at the end of the day, it doesn't change the basics of it. My daughter has all the symptoms of schizophrenia. It can be managed like any other illness. Like any other illness there will be good times and bad. All we can do is take it as it comes, love her every moment, and try to understand and then advocate for her.

I have always known our healthcare system was broken, but never did I understand it so much as I do now. No one can until they experience it. The mental illness and health challenges facing families across the country and the world are terrifying. We will be caregivers for our daughter all her life until we die. Then what? If she outlives us (which statistically is against the odds, but I have been going against those all my life and I hope Libby will too), who will take care of her? If I died tomorrow, what would happen to her? The thought terrifies me because there is no one. My husband has no legal rights as a stepparent. Will she be homeless and lost in a world of horrors with no respite from them, with no one to love and soothe her from her living nightmare?

My husband doesn't understand the connection Libby and I share and to be quite honest, neither do I. I shared a piece of my heart, body, and soul with her which forged a bond like no other. There's nothing I wouldn't do for her. I live because of my love for her. She saved me from my own demons just by her creation. I have no doubt she was meant to be here, and I was meant to be her mother. Loving her, knowing her, and being there for her has changed me so fundamentally and completely, who I used to be is a dream of some other person.

What to do with that? I have the tools and making to be a mental health advocate, but how to start? How to do that with everything else that's going on? I need to build my real estate business and give my husband a platform from which he can launch from into a new career. I need to take care of Libby and Phoenix, who has issues of his own.

My plate is already full, is there room for anything else? The time for change needs to be now. So many people suffer from mental illness. It's affecting countless families with a huge ripple effect. It cannot continue to be ignored. How many children like Libby could be lifted out of the depths of mental illness, but fall through the cracks due to ignorance and a healthcare system full of holes?

I will be leaving my job soon and leaping back into self-employment again. I only hope I can fly fast enough and high enough to lift us all.

September 15, 2018

DOUBLING DOWN

I am relieved to share that Libby seems to be out of her psychosis and stabilizing. They more than doubled the antipsychotics to bring her back to reality. She's out of acute care and back in the residential program. We believe the middle school environment with all its triggers to be a large reason for her relapse, along with not enough support from her outpatient team. We are working to figure out a plan forward for her, and I am working to find a new psychiatrist and therapist again. I also am working with the school district to find a solution, which may involve a transfer to a smaller charter school.

Thanks everyone for the support and encouragement, it was and is appreciated! I am working to get myself back on track as well.

October 2, 2018

NO IMPROVEMENT

I am sorry to say Libby has not improved in the last thirty days. We thought she was but her psychosis hovers closely, and there's no identifiable triggers. We are now looking at six months as a minimum stay. We had a difficult discussion Monday with her therapist after our visit this weekend, about being unable to care for Libby at home with her symptoms. She has devolved so completely from six months ago.

Libby's hallucinations have changed into a killer clown, which I am sad to say is a common hallucination for people with schizophrenia. What's worse is if going to a restaurant for a meal is all it takes to bring on psychosis, the veil for her is too thin. She cannot function at school. For the first time we used the words, "We can't take care of her in our home any longer."

I cannot express the heartbreak. I no longer know what the future holds. I am just trying to hold myself together. I am trying to accept that my daughter may be gone for much longer than we would like or may not be able to come home at all. We thought we would have more time. We are fortunate - we have resources. Libby is getting treatment. My husband and I are focusing on our relationship, and each other, to help us through. I would be utterly lost without him.

October 4, 2018

RESILIENCE

I learned recently about this amazing thing we humans have: resilience. It's what gives us the ability to bounce back from tragedy, fight through hardship, and keep fighting through our struggles. Everyone's resilience is diffcrent.

Unfortunately, Libby's resilience doesn't work like everyone else's. Events in life are like a shock to her and she doesn't seem to have the ability or strength to overcome them. My resilience has seen me through numerous tragedies and terrible circumstances. It's what keeps me going now as I am tested in new ways.

How do you teach resilience? How do you learn and develop it? How do you teach it to an 11-year-old? It's not fair to expect everyone to have the same resilience or expect everyone will weather life's troubles in the same way.

October 14, 2018

THE WHY OF IT ALL

As people have likely been wondering lately why I am posting so much about my personal life, I am going to share the reasons now.

1. No one can know someone's story just by looking at them. One CANNOT know. Many of my colleagues are surprised when they hear about the struggles our family has and are dealing with. Four out of four of our family members have mental health issues. I, for one, refuse to be ashamed or hide it, because that's part of the problem. I don't need to hang a sign around my neck and declare it, but I should be able to say the words PTSD, Depression, Autism, or Schizophrenia like any other diagnosis, and not fear being mistreated!

2. I have lost friends, I have lost family, and I have lost opportunities because of sharing our situation.

However, I refuse to stop. Why? It is important! We need to be more accepting of the invisible pain inside each of us. We need to be lifting each other up and supporting each other. I am so proud of the people who have reached out to me in support. We thank you for it.

3. My support system's support, acknowledgement, and encouragement has meant the world to me. It has given me strength when I needed it most. Every message, every prayer, every hug from me a friend, every lunch date to distract me and connect me with new friends, every time someone has checked to see how they can help, has been a gift. My friends are everywhere, scattered around the world, and I cherish each of them. While Facebook gets a bad rap for being what it is, this connection would not be possible without this platform. Facebook is just the tool, it's how each one of us choose to use it that matters. I have been using it for over a decade. I have held classes and taught people how to use it safely, effectively, and proficiently. I am happy to teach it again. If people want to share vile things with the world, that's their choice, but what comes around goes around on Facebook so I hope what people put out there is kind. I choose to be open, honest, and as kind on Facebook as I try to be in real life. I just try to love everyone. Our world so desperately needs love and healing. If a kind word or gesture can help do that, I will do it all day and never tire of it.

4. I am hurting right now, have no doubt. Every breath I take is hard right now. I share this pain not to gain sympathy or pity. Please don't feel sorry for me, or us. I share it to give others courage and strength. Watch - we will beat this; all of it. I love this little family we have built, and WE WILL NOT FAIL. I will love and support and help them always; it's the promise I have made. I can't fix what is wrong, but I can love, listen, wipe tears, and offer help. I can try to understand, protect, and give my family a safe place to come to. I can share our story, so others can learn. I can write articles and books, teach what I have learned, and try to make it easier for someone else. I can open up on Facebook, and in conversations with others, to try to start some change.

5. I get a lot of questions lately about how people can help. Believe it or not, that question alone is a great start. A desire to help is amazing and means a person cares. Unfortunately, there's not a lot of ways to help. My biggest problem right now is getting my house clean. One way to help is to donate through PayPal. It's going to cost a lot of money, because I physically can't clean our home. Today is $115. I expect to spend about $500 cleaning and rearranging to make this place a bit more handicap accessible. I am trying to figure out a solution for the bathroom shower so my husband doesn't fall, because he cannot feel his left leg and his arms are weakening. We don't own the house, so I

have to be careful. Another way to help is referrals. I am looking for magazines and newspapers to write for, as well as clients to help buy, sell, or lease property. I am a mobile notary, so opportunity to do that is great.

6. Most of all, be nice to others. Forget about what divides us and work to be closer to each other. Help one another and listen a little more. Our country is so sure its opinion is the right, and only, one. We are missing the point, which is to work together to solve the problem, to overcome our differences and find our strengths together. We can't get anything solved by fighting. Our forefathers knew that and would be ashamed that we missed their message.

I love all of you. No matter where you are. No matter what you believe. No matter how well I know you. Thank you for reading and supporting us. I hope it inspires you to go fight your own battles and love fiercely.

October 19, 2018

WHAT NEXT?

Hubby is home, but meds have him unable to drive. He needs to be closely supervised until his body acclimates to meds. Phoenix got kicked out of his Partial Hospitalization Program (PHP) program for triggering other kids deliberately. I mean, really? What next? I am exhausted!

FALLING APART TO BUILD AGAIN

This update will be quick, as I'm riding in a vehicle to go see Libby for the first time in a month. The meds seem to be finally helping, and she's finally not hearing and seeing things. She also no longer believes everyone is trying to kill her.

In the meantime, everything else in our life fell apart in rapid fashion. My son had to be admitted for a desire to hurt himself. We found out about some physical abuse Phoenix experienced four years ago, which triggered a CPS investigation and criminal investigation against my husband's ex-wife and her best friend. He was inpatient for a week.

The day Phoenix got out, my husband admitted to wanting to kill himself and had a plan. I picked up my son and then had to call a crisis team for Robert. Watching him be escorted by two sheriff's officers was a whole new low. The precipitating factor was my husband recognizing his symptoms may be worsening.

Our household now has three disabled individuals in it. This is proving to be a difficult transition for me to navigate. Instead of my husband overseeing the household, it's now falling to me, and I am responsible for three dependents. This is not what I envisioned for my life at all. I don't resent it, but I am so scared of the future. Our journey continues to evolve and grow more complicated. I'm working to transition into real estate full time and out of my Paralegal position by the end of the year.

October 22, 2018

LOSING IT

Ok, so here's the latest: Robert is home but his ability to function is coming and going. He has fallen twice now, which scares me to death. We may need nursing help if this keeps up. On top of that, Libby may be getting released.

We saw Libby yesterday. The psychosis has eased somewhat thanks to her time on the unit, but she has regressed so much mentally that she doesn't even remember how to do simple math. She doesn't remember the last few months.

Returning to school is going to be so much fun. I have her annual Admission, Review and Dismissal (ARD) meeting tomorrow, where they will tell me how much Libby has fallen behind and what her new accommodations need to be. I am trying desperately to find a resource that can teach her from home. She is now on 3.5mg daily of Risperdal, divided up into three doses a day.

My heart breaks that Libby needs that much of this medication to function now. She has gained a ton of weight, and is now 120 lbs. We are going to try and get her into an exercise program or something. A Medicaid representative came to the house last week, who has experience with schizophrenia in kids. When I described Libby she said, "your daughter is broken, and she always will be, but she can learn to function around it". As a parent, that is so hard because she laughs, talks, smiles, and does all these things that if one doesn't know her well, one would never know she is broken inside.

Phoenix is home and has barely improved. Cedar Crest is such a joke - they didn't even give us his new meds. I am fighting with them about that.

October 24, 2018

ONE STEP FORWARD, TWO STEPS BACK

Latest update: Robert's neurologist appointment was today. They have ordered a brain, neck, and upper back MRI, lab work, and a nerve conduction study. He has lost reflexes in his knees and elbows. He's also lost sensation in his left leg and left toes.

October 28, 2018

FAILING & REGROUPING

How many times will I have to work to rebuild our lives? How many times can one family fail to move forward? We've made strides over the last four years but in general, our family fails to thrive due to a whole host of medical issues. Stability is a laughable term. There's always something going on, whether it be a crisis, concern, or problem. I feel like I'm living a soap opera sometimes.

My husband's health is mysteriously deteriorating and we're struggling to find answers as to why. We suspect Multiple Sclerosis and are waiting on a series of tests to help us determine what's going on. In the meantime, I'm fighting with Libby's facility to continue her treatment. They claim she's doing well on the unit, and there's no medical need to keep her there, yet she is suicidal and hallucinating in the classroom. I don't believe the unit is documenting her issues properly.

Robert decided yesterday that we needed a smaller living space so that he can move around easier and so we can maintain it easier. We're going to purchase an RV to live in for the next year, as well as a truck so we can travel wherever we need to. We'll hopefully buy some land eventually that we can put an RV hook up on and live off of that. Temporarily we'll live out of an RV park.

We'll also be bringing both kids home, so we can educate them outside of the school system. I'm sick of these idiotic people not listening to me with regard to what our kids need. I'm tired of watching my child be pushed into psychosis because of others. I'm tired of fighting the school system, and my kids still not being able to progress because they don't fit into the cookie cutter system. Elementary school was hard for both of my kids, but middle school has been utterly impossible. I'm done wasting time and energy on a system that doesn't care. I may not know the first thing about teaching but by God, I will learn. I will do whatever it takes to help these two kids grow, develop, and learn to the best of their abilities. No one else may care, but I certainly do.

In addition, I'm leaving my full-time job as a Paralegal and going into real estate full time. I've changed brokerages to make it easier for me to achieve that. They will provide leads for me to work, along with building my business. Hopefully, all of these changes will make it easier for us financially. I've missed more work in the last two weeks than I ever have.

The future is looking a little more optimistic with these changes, but it's all still very scary. I'm hopeful we can find a way to make all this work somehow.

October 28, 2018

MENTAL HEALTH & MINDFULNESS

My therapist has told me each day I am to spend an hour doing something to relax myself, something fun and just for me. It's usually either painting or coloring, sometimes writing if I have the mental ability. I sometimes blog as well.

The past week I have worked on this at the beginning and end of the day. This is colored with fine point pens and gel pens. Each color represents something, below is the breakdown.

- Yellow = hope & optimism for the future
- Blue = peace and tranquility
- Pink = love
- Red = anger, frustration
- Green = rebirth
- Purple = pain, sorrow, grief

Loosely this translates into: please fill our lives with hope, optimism, peace, tranquility, and love to fend off the anger, frustration, grief, and pain we are enduring.

What kind of things do YOU do to help yourself each day? Life can be stressful and needs an outlet.

October 31, 2018

WISHES & HOPES FOR 2018

I realized something today in a moment of clarity. Unbidden, while following the ambulance with Robert in it, praying every mile that the lights wouldn't come on, an image rose into my mind of what life would be like for Phoenix, Libby, and Robert if I weren't here.

Phoenix would go to his biological mom, who can't even take care of herself, has been diagnosed with bipolar disorder and schizophrenia, and gave up her son to his father. Libby would be a ward of the state. Robert would be lost in a system he is not capable of managing, and possibly homeless.

Without me, these people whom I love more than anything would suffer in agony and despair. Somehow, some way, we were brought together. I am where I am meant to be. There is a purpose here that is greater than I can understand.

I will not falter. I will not fail, no matter what it takes. The alternative is far, far worse. Somehow, it has put things into a different kind of perspective. Love each other every moment. It can be gone in a blink.

Facebook is turning into a little bit of a journal for me to record the snippets, the moments that are important, because I don't have a lot of time to blog.

November 2, 2018

SCORE ONE FOR THE GOOD GUYS

Score one for the good guys! I went up against BCBSTX, with two appeals through her doctor, which has gotten Libby additional treatment. It's likely to only be 5-7 days, but I will take it. It looks like all my strong advocating and her clear need for treatment worked! I am so relieved for her. I think every day she is there gives her a little more inner strength, which she will need.

November 2, 2018

CAN I PLEASE GET A BREAK?

We are having to admit Phoenix again, this time for suicidal thoughts and self-harming. He scraped the skin off the top of his fingers.

November 3, 2018

CHICKEN TENDERS

Today was a mixed bag. Robert woke up overwhelmed and disassociated. I had to go see Libby, and with everything that happened this week, Robert is on suicide watch again. His words: "I can't take anymore." I get it, but I couldn't leave him alone all day. It took me over an hour to get him out of bed, showered, dressed, and in the car. We went to Copperas Cove, then on to San Antonio.

Libby did amazing. We did our best to expose her to everything we could that could trigger her, so that was dinner and a movie ("The Nutcracker and the Four Realms").

Little did I know it had such triggers in it for her (multiple clowns and mice plus a certain creepy factor). But as far as I could tell she did great. I took her to the bathroom and then the second time had her go on her own. She found her way back fine. We updated her on all the news from home, including Robert's condition. She cried but seemed to recover well. She seems very lucid and verbalized her coping skills with confidence. At this point, we may just have to bring her home and see what happens. At the same time, Libby didn't know what chicken tenders were...

November 5, 2018

COUNT YOUR BLESSINGS

I had a brief medical exam today to renew prescriptions, and amazingly enough: my blood pressure is perfect. Robert almost fell over in disbelief. With all the stress, at least my heart's still good! He battles chronic high blood pressure and is overweight. I'm overweight too, but no blood pressure problems. Am I just lucky? We'll go with blessed.

November 6, 2018

COMING HOME

It looks like Libby is coming home by Friday! Phoenix remains hospitalized, but hopefully we will all be together for the holidays. I'm so excited, and so nervous. This time people actually listened to me, so there's a transition plan. Medicaid has provided two counselors for outpatient treatment who work with psychosis. Thanks to the Thanksgiving holiday, Libby will have two weeks at home without school, so she can re-acclimate to things here. I have a meeting with school administration next week, to come up with a transition plan to put in effect immediately. I reached out to the school's special education director, to get her involved, because both of my kids are being mishandled. She has been very responsive.

We have an MRI and an EEG pending for Robert this week, but I now think Cymbalta may have been worsening his possible MS symptoms. We are weaning him off it, and he has shown signs of his former self. He is not 100% but is experiencing fewer seizing spasms. If I can get a diagnosis and get him on his feet, I think I will have the bases covered. Finances remain a little uncertain, but hopefully only for a few more days, while a commission check is being processed.

It's been a grueling month, but I have some hope again that the worst might be past for now. Amidst all this, my real estate business has been humming right along. I have no closings scheduled yet, but more opportunities than I have ever had in my career. Having a $10 million pipeline is amazing, and I just recently began working with a client with a $4 million budget. Super exciting!

My therapist said recently that my resilience has bounced back faster than he has ever seen for a person in this much crisis and I'm grateful for that. We went to programs for help and found none available, but when I went to friends, we were immensely blessed with kindness from all around.

November 7, 2018

COMING HOME PART II

This Friday Libby should be getting released to come home. It's been over two months since we admitted her. To be honest, I'm a bit nervous. Every time we bring her home it's different, and there are challenges. This time is a bit worse, because I'm bringing home a child with the mentality of a nearly six-year-old and putting her into a hostile environment at the school.

This school, which has been chewing up and spitting out my kids for the last three months, is no place for my kids. Phoenix has gone back inpatient for the second time in thirty days because of the environment there. I finally called the special education coordinator for the district and got her involved. I'm done playing nice with this school, and we're working to find a way to bring them home and school them. I don't care about all these stupid ideas they have about the school environment being best for them.

For my kids it's a pressure cooker, and I can only catch them so many times before I will miss, or they won't come to me.

LATER

My husband and I discussed it in detail and decided we're going to make the leap and homeschool the kids. We cannot risk the school continuing to mentally break and torture them. We'll see how that goes, and whether they start to progress both educationally and mentally. Maybe getting them out of the school environment will give them what they need. Lord knows, I'm running out of options at this point, and we're not even sure if Libby is even capable of learning anymore.

November 7, 2018

SEIZURES CONTINUE

Robert has been having seizure-like spasms since November 1. We've gone to the ER already, once by ambulance. He had five long episodes today. Last night, for the first time, his legs wouldn't work. He couldn't stand for about 20 minutes. Strength eventually came back, but every day it gets a little worse.

Whatever this is, I am watching it take him piece by piece. Robert has given me full power of attorney over him, in case he becomes incapacitated. I am starting to lose hope that we can stop this. He said the words brain tumor to me today, and everything stopped. I have been unwilling to even consider it.

I have been bartering with God for weeks. I will accept MS, or Parkinson's, if it just means we have more time. Every time I watch him in an episode there's a darkness there, like something awful has a hold on him and is twisting him. He's starting to lose his short-term memory. If I lose him, I lose Phoenix too. It's more than I can bear to consider, but he is making plans. He thinks this could be terminal. Against my will, I am starting to wonder if he's right.

November 9, 2018

THREE CUPS

Robert is in the hospital waiting for his EEG still and will be until they have one free. No discharge for Phoenix yet, as they can't get his meds right. I am on my way to get Libby and bring her home. Has anyone ever seen those carnival games with the three cups, and one has to guess where the ball is to win a prize? That's my life right now! The cups just keep shuffling. We haven't had a day with everyone home together since Labor Day. I don't know how I am even able to do all of this.

November 11, 2018

RESULTS ARE IN

The result from the EEG was a diagnosis of non-epileptic seizures. I didn't even know that was a thing. It is not caused by electrical activity in the brain. We are being referred to another specialist for neuropsychology. This is the strangest damn thing I have ever heard of. The medical mystery continues.

November 12, 2018

TOO BUSY TO LOSE IT

Another hectic day. I went to therapy (not much help), then we had some dear friends come help clean. We got Phoenix's room completely cleaned and his bathroom. I cannot even express how grateful I am for that because while they did that, I got a call that they were discharging Phoenix today and I had to get him by midnight. No warning, no discharge plan, nothing. I've been trying to talk to the psychiatrist since he was admitted with no luck.

We're going to watch him for the next couple days to see how he does but already his anxiety is higher because all his stuff is rearranged. He's still unstable. They also took him off his ADHD meds completely. Cold turkey. So now I have an autistic un-medicated ADHD depressed child who self-harms in a chaotic environment with a child with psychosis and two adults with PTSD. This should go really well...

He put a six inch or better scratch down his arm with his fingernails while in the facility. Then told them he wants to self-harm because he was in the facility. Talk about learning what buttons to push! We may have to put him into the facility that Libby treated at some time later this week for longer treatment. Sometimes I think these facilities do more harm than good.

Tomorrow I have two MHMR appts for the kids, a fridge to sell, and a bunch of properties to show. All before noon. I was also blessed today to get an opportunity for a new listing of a historical home, so I'll be working on that too (and she's a beauty too!)

How do I keep my sanity? I'm too busy to lose it!

November 13, 2018

ALL UNDER ONE ROOF

For the first time since Labor Day, everyone is under one roof. We are rapidly putting our plan into action for moving into an RV. I have just about everything listed online for sale now and have already sold some tools. We have some big stuff that needs to be sold, but hopefully it will all happen in the next 45 days.

November 18, 2018

IMPROVEMENTS

Robert's medical mystery might be somewhat solved. I weaned Robert off Cymbalta 2 weeks ago. His symptoms showed immediate improvement. He now has been a week without a seizure, and his strength is returning. He has resumed his other meds with no issues. He has been able to resume his normal routine again, including some short driving. He is still having underlying neurological symptoms, but they are more manageable, so we think Cymbalta was intensifying what's going on neurologically. I really hate that drug, always have. I'm glad Robert is getting some of his life back. We still have to solve the issue that remains, which is what's going on neurologically. He has a neuropsychiatric test on 12/4 for six hours. Maybe that will give some answers.

November 19, 2018

WEIRD PLACES

Another update: things have reached a weird place. Libby is in and out of psychosis throughout the day, and we are baffled as to how to keep her stable. Libby is slowly escalating, and having trouble remembering who we are. There is almost nothing worse than your child looking at you and asking, "Who are you? Why am I here? Where am I?" I don't know how long we will be able to keep her home and safe. Phoenix is also in a weird place, and we are on the verge of admitting him for residential treatment as well. Multiple years without proper autism interventions has reduced him to medium functioning, and we are having a hard time getting through to him.

As a mom, I hate watching my kids break repeatedly. The instinct is for them to be healthy and happy. It's part of my job as a parent and I feel like I am failing them both, despite doing everything I can think to.

November 22, 2018

BIRTHDAY WISH LIST

- Amazon gift card so I can get books for my Kindle. The new Jack Reacher book is out, and I can't afford it
- Texas Roadhouse for dinner.
- Movie tickets so I can see the new "Fantastic Beasts" movie, "Bumblebee," and "How to Train Your Dragon" (with the kids).

Hopefully I can make enough tips through working for Uber, Lyft, and Favor to have some fun! We were able to get Robert his birthday and Christmas presents (two video games), thanks to a friend paying us for a handyman job. We are still working on gifts for the kids (they are so hard to shop for now!), but we got them each a writing tablet a little early. 29 days and counting until I turn 39! 33 days until Christmas.

November 24, 2018

ADMITTED

I got Phoenix admitted last night and didn't get done until 12:30 a.m. Robert stayed home with Libby. I checked into the hotel about 1, fell asleep at 2, and was back awake at 7:45. Now I am off to do some Uber/Lyft/Favor runs in San Antonio to pay for the gas and hotel. I need to earn about $200 today.

November 25, 2018

BEHAVING BADLY

There is one bit of good news. Phoenix behaved so badly on his first day, the weekend therapist called me to discuss it. Apparently, he came close to starting a fight in group and had to be removed. This is the same crap he does here at home. He is in competent hands now.

Unfortunately, if this doesn't work, we aren't sure what to do next. Military school? His mom? We can't have Phoenix disrupting the house and deliberately triggering Libby (which is a form of emotional and verbal abuse). Now we wait and see what happens. I know they have their hands full, because we certainly have. We are hoping we get answers quickly, but I am guessing he is going to need residential treatment for a month.

November 27, 2018

I HATE IT HERE

I am not sure why, but every day just seems to be getting a little harder. Phoenix is not doing well inpatient and refuses to cooperate. He is steadily escalating in risk and his answer is, "I hate it here". I am sorry, but you hate it at home too. You asked me to take you there!

What are we supposed to do? We are making plans to possibly send Phoenix temporarily to his biological mom. Maybe she can figure something out with him, or at least give him a break from the stress. We are running out of options for him. The treatment team refuses to give him meds, because they say it's all behavioral and due to the choices he is making, that he is actively refusing to follow the rules and stop harming himself. He says harming himself feels good.

I just don't know anymore. I am doing something wrong to have two kids this messed up, but I will be damned if I can figure out what. I feel like the worst mother on Earth, but all I am doing is trying to love them and help them. Libby, for the moment, is doing well. She still hallucinates several times a day, but we work through her coping skills and they pass. She seems happy to be home.

November 29, 2018

PERSISTENCE

Finally, persistence and prayers win the day! I talked to the psychiatrist. They are going to wean Phoenix off the Zoloft. The theory is he's experiencing a side effect of aggression and agitation from the medicine, especially when they increased it to 150mg (hence his escalation recently). They are going to try a different medication and recommend for Residential Treatment Center (RTC). This is so they can work on the behavioral issues he is displaying and try to get his anxiety under control.

I hated having Phoenix on Zoloft, as it counteracted his ADHD meds too. Unfortunately, I have learned the hard way that providers will report you to CPS for medical neglect if a medication is prescribed for a child, but you stop giving it. I had to have a doctor decide. I am so glad it was her idea, and not what I have been asking about for the past week.

Fingers crossed - hopefully Phoenix will be here in time for the New Year.

A SWEET, SWEET DAY

I spent most of the day with Libby yesterday. We took a road trip and it was such a sweet, simple day. I pointed out things that I knew would delight her - a goat farm, a train, cows, pretty trees. Her delight filled the car. It hit home to me that for her, life will likely never progress past that of being six years old. At 11, almost 12, she's literally stuck as a six-year-old. Some concepts are just beyond her ability to understand now, and at times I forget. I look at her and see a budding young lady. It's such a strange dichotomy.

Case in point: I used the word proof in a sentence and Libby asked what it meant. I explained it and gave some simple examples. Then, I asked her if she could come up with an example of proof. She was baffled, so I tried to help her. I pointed to the sky and said what color is that? She said blue. I asked, "What's your proof?" She couldn't tell me it was because she could see the color with her eyes. Abstract concepts are just so beyond her. I honestly don't know how we are going to educate her. We have her at a first-grade level, and that's slow going when it should be easy. She learned it once, but it's all brand new to her now. That's a heartbreak in itself. I have had to shift my perspective to what she's capable of, instead of what I hoped for her. As a mom, that's hard to do.

Meanwhile Phoenix was violent on the unit again, flipping tables and chairs. Maybe it gives him a safe place to express his rage at life. It must seem as unfair to him as it does to us. They are going to give him meds for agitation, finally. I have requested six times to talk to the psychiatrist, with no results, but that's par for the course.

Robert is struggling, and I don't know how to help him. He's still having seizures, but they haven't gone past a two of ten. We are waiting on medication recommendations from the specialist. His birthday is today, and I have to find a way to make it a good day for him. I am taking today off and leaving my phone on "do not disturb," so I can focus on him. I'm hoping his mood will be less volatile than it has been.

December 5, 2018

EXTRA! EXTRA! READ ALL ABOUT IT!

FINALLY! I could just dance and cry with relief. I think we finally have an outpatient medical home for Libby as of today with MHMR. We did an intake, and the psychiatrist was so compassionate and kind. It took over three hours, but he was amazing. He confirmed everything we have suspected. H let me know that no one in the practice can diagnose schizophrenia in a child younger than 13, and that it's a licensing issue. Clinicians have to be specially licensed for it, and the official diagnosis is generally made at ages 13 and up. It's extremely rare for a child to be so severe at her age.

All of this we knew but having someone care enough to confirm and explain it was so helpful! Libby is textbook schizophrenia. The doctor knew it just looking at her! I couldn't believe it. He said he identified it within two minutes of talking to her. There is no doubt, and that's as close as I am going to get at this stage. Finally, I can stop battling for a diagnosis, focus on some other things, and just wait.

Libby has a new therapist, and I had a chance to meet her. For the first time ever in her treatment other than inpatient, I was invited to be in the therapy sessions to help. Oh my God! I could have hugged him. She's going to receive the highest level of services they offer, which includes in home services. It will take some time to set up.

The social worker also let me know that there's group homes that we can send Libby to, if inpatient fails and she can no longer be at home. I pray that doesn't become necessary, but he was very honest that he's never seen a case as severe as hers, at such a young age, improve drastically enough to allow her to be self-sufficient. The best we can hope for is that between meds and therapy, we can keep her stable enough to live with us. The breaking line will come if she becomes a physical danger to us or herself. We are not set up for that, and until we are in the RV, it isn't possible to be.

The social worker has significant experience with psychosis. Libby had a hallucination in his office, which gave him some real insight. He will be working with her as well, and seemed genuinely interested in her case and care.

I am grateful for the prayers and support. I think a big piece of our puzzle just fell into place. Now I just need to get an MRI for Libby to prove the cognitive loss, and we will be all set for the time being. I have a doctor's appointment with her on 12/17 to hopefully discuss that.

Finally, I can scratch this off my to-do list. As a parent and a child advocate, I felt I needed to fight as much as necessary to get Libby a proper diagnosis, and so that's what I have been doing.

Now that I know there's an age at which full diagnosis becomes possible, and they can do it at our provider's office when Libby is old enough, I can refocus that mental energy elsewhere for a while. I can focus on real estate, writing, Robert, Phoenix, getting the RV, or whatever else there is. I have been obsessed with Libby's treatment and getting a proper diagnosis for so long, it's like a giant weight is lifted off my chest. Such relief!

December 17, 2018

RELAPSED AGAIN

Libby is inpatient again. It's 2:30 a.m. and I'm exhausted. I will share more details later today; first, to sleep.

*** LATER THAT DAY ***

Libby's admitted again. It took nine hours, but it was a pretty easy case to make. I refuse to be disheartened, because we're getting better at this. I believe if we just keep at it, we will find a way to properly manage this. An interesting thing happened while she was being admitted. The doctor mentioned that Libby's diagnosis had been changed to schizoaffective disorder with depressive mood. I wasn't aware her diagnosis had officially changed, so I'll be calling tomorrow to verify. That's potentially a step in the right direction for her in terms of a diagnosis. If nothing else, it would at least confirm what I've been suspecting for over two years.

December 17, 2018

REFLECTIONS ON PROGRESS

Yesterday, December 16, 2018, marked yet another admission for Libby. It had been coming for over a week, but I selfishly didn't want to let her go. She's only been home a month this time. Every time she leaves it's like a part of me goes with her, and I can't be whole until she's home again. We made the three-hour trip to San Antonio, went through a nine-hour admission process full of waiting, and then I drove the three hours home. All told, I didn't get home until 2:30 a.m. I didn't fall asleep until 3:30, and then got up at 6:30 for an interview. Today is also the one-year anniversary of me starting this blog. How far we've come in such a short time. Yet, so far to go, but that's a post for another entry.

So much has happened recently, I hardly know where to begin. For a while, Libby was really improved, then the hallucinations returned. They gradually got worse and started keeping her up at night. They started happening when she was sleeping or awake. Other symptoms gradually came back. She wanted to kill herself. She had visions of slitting her own throat. She had hallucinations tell her she would die in her sleep, which made her terrified to go to sleep. The auditory hallucinations returned for the first time since January. Through it all, though, Libby kept her composure, mostly. She cried a lot. There were moments that were like a rainbow after the rain. We went on road trips. We had Quizno's, her new favorite restaurant. We played, cuddled, read stories, watched movies, and talked. Oh, how we talked, about everything. I started teaching her things again - vocabulary, things about life, history, science. She was full of questions about everything. She'd lost so much knowledge from the psychosis, which lasted almost 3 months.

Then Phoenix broke. Bad. He started self-harming, scratching himself with his nails. I never knew you could do that kind of damage with fingernails. Six inches long on his forearms, and deep, knuckle to knuckle on his fingers. We admitted him three times in 30 days for treatment. He just kept getting kicked out of places. He was kicked out of one facility into a partial hospitalization program. That lasted four days. He was deliberately triggering other kids and not following the rules. I pleaded with the staff, "how can you kick him out for that? He's there to get help!"

They did it anyway. I filed a complaint with the facility that went nowhere. Lost in a crisis and trying to get Phoenix help, we tried a facility in Austin, an hour away. He lasted a week, then told the staff he was hurting himself because he was in the facility, so they too kicked him out. I wanted to scream. Between my two kids, he's the less severe, but we couldn't find help for him any easier than we had for her. Then he deliberately triggered Libby again.

I had a therapy session that day, Robert had a doctor's appointment. We were five minutes apart, so Robert left, and I headed home. We talked about me going to the pharmacy real quick on my way home, but I decided it wasn't important enough to leave the kids alone. Thank God something in me said to get home. I pulled in the driveway and heard a scream from our house. I didn't even shut the car door or turn it off I bolted for the house. I burst through the door to find Libby sobbing and shaking. The words tumbled out of her mouth. "Oh thank God! Mommy! Phoenix told me a masked man was coming up the driveway and going to get us."

I have known rage like that one other time before and it was also because of Phoenix. He'd called Libby crazy to her face, reducing her to hysterical tears. I told him then if he ever did it again, he would never live in the same house as Libby and me again. Now he'd done it again.

I lit into Phoenix verbally, shaking with pure rage and adrenaline, while trying to comfort Libby. We have told him time and time again: don't trigger her; don't antagonize her; don't use her weaknesses against her; don't mess with her head! There will be terrible consequences if you do. For a while it worked, and then suddenly he didn't care anymore. No matter how much we try to give them both equal attention, it's never enough. And what's worse, Libby adores him. All she wants is for Phoenix to be a big brother to her. He's either unable or unwilling to even be kind to her. He doesn't even tolerate her. Try as we might, we can't get through to him.

Five minutes was all it took, and he would have instigated a full-on panic attack in a girl with paranoid schizophrenia, with violent tendencies when triggered. He did it on purpose again. I called Robert, explained the situation, and he too lost it a bit. Unfortunately, he was at the doctor's office to do blood work but couldn't because his blood pressure was through the roof. They feared a heart attack. I'd inadvertently triggered him as well.

By the time Robert got home, I'd come down to a simmering boil of rage, instead of a volcanic eruption of it. Robert was ready to beat Phoenix and send him to his biological mom. I intervened and mediated. Listening to Phoenix beg for one more chance broke my heart, but I get it. I was there with Libby two years ago. Sometimes when one doesn't have any idea what to do, everything one tries fails or blows up in one's face, it just seems like giving up is the only option. One runs out of ideas, options, patience, and hope.

I stood my ground. Even though Phoenix isn't legally mine, in my heart he's my son, and I made a promise to him five years ago to be his mom. I did the only thing I could. I took Phoenix to the same place Libby was treated. I let him know this was his last opportunity to get help and help himself. We had a long talk on the way there (there were three hours to kill after all). Phoenix put me through hell for over twelve hours in the admissions office, triggering me in every way he could. It was psychological torture and afterward, I was so mentally drained and exhausted I couldn't drive home. It was after midnight anyway, so I got a hotel room. I hadn't thought to bring my meds, not expecting to be there that long, so I didn't have my anxiety meds or anything to help me sleep.

Fortunately, exhaustion did the trick for about six hours, then I was up bright and early at 7:30 a.m. The plan was to run for Uber, Lyft, and Favor in San Antonio to pay for the expense of the trip there and the hotel room. I needed to make about $200. Unfortunately, I forgot I was in the wrong vehicle for Uber and Lyft, so that left Favor. While I'm familiar with San Antonio, I'm not THAT familiar with it. Combined with my anxiety and PTSD symptoms from no meds and the night before, I was such a wreck I finally had to give up around noon and head home. My body felt like someone was sending electric shocks through me repeatedly, and the nerve endings all over my body were jangling like bells. I made $40.

When I got home, I took my anxiety meds. It would take three days to recover from Phoenix's onslaught. I love him, but in the last two years we've learned that he's smart enough to manipulate others. Worse, he likes to trigger people and see their reactions, good or bad, regardless of consequences. Time will tell whether or not he will come back to live with us. At this point, his mother is ready and willing to take him, as are his grandparents. We're ready to send him, at least on a provisional basis. It would give him and us a much-needed break. If it works out better for him, great. If not, we'll bring him back when Mom has had enough and try again. At the end of the day we want to help him, but he has to want to help himself. So far, we're not seeing any desire to do so, even while he's inpatient. Unfortunately for Phoenix, his previous shenanigans won't work there. They know exactly what to do with him there and are enforcing some very strict guidelines. He's miserable, but until he figures out how to behave properly, that's where he's staying. Let him give them hell for a while. Maybe while they are at it, they can figure out what the hell his issues are and solve some of them.

Amongst all this chaos, if you can believe it, I interviewed for a job and am expecting an offer anytime. Fingers crossed that I'll get hired this week, because we need money in the worst way. Our plans to finance the RV fell through without a co-signer, and we haven't been able to raise the $10-20K down payment we need. Our lease is up in June, so I'm taking a multi-faceted approach to the problem. I have enough money to pay January rent and a car payment. That's it. The phone bill is past due, insurance is canceled, and I don't know where gas money will come from. Real estate has slowed down tremendously. My last team lead told me December was the biggest month of the year for real estate. He was full of crap. I probably won't sell anything again until next year. For now, I'm just enjoying life and doing my best NOT to panic. Do not panic. I will not panic. This job will be the answer to a prayer.

Getting a full-time job making at least $40K a year + selling real estate will hopefully give us the cash we need to put down on the RV. I should be able to make about $100K next year. In the meantime, we are selling everything that isn't nailed down. We are packing, discarding, reorganizing, and preparing to downsize into a 41' home on wheels. I cannot wait Libby and Robert can't either. This place we are in is too big and too expensive. At least this way, one day we'll own something. We've paid $36,000 in rent and have no assets to show for it. At that rate, we'll pay the RV off in 5 years (it would be financed for 10).

December 17, 2018

WHY CHILDHOOD SCHIZOPHRENIA IS SO HARD

I'm very active in several schizophrenia groups online and on Facebook. When I tell people on these forums that my child is 11 and has schizophrenia, their tone changes. When I tell people Libby has had symptoms for over six years, they're shocked. Justifiably so.

Schizophrenia is already one of the worst and most debilitating mental illnesses facing humanity, and in a child, it's a tragedy. The outcome for that population is even dimmer than the already dim potential outcomes for adults. Let me break it down for you:

An estimated 1.1% of adults in America (2.2 million) are living with schizophrenia (SCZ). Now think of that for a moment. That means they're surrounded by 99% of people who don't understand or have a frame of reference for their disability. It's not so much that it's worse than anything else out there, it's that it's rare. An estimated 51 million people have schizophrenia. That's two times more than Alzheimer's, five times more than multiple sclerosis, six times more than insulin-dependent diabetes, and 60 times more than muscular dystrophy, per schizophrenia.com. To find rarity like that, you'd have to look at AIDS which is 0.8% of the world's population.

For an idea of possible outcomes, here's a breakdown:

- *25% Completely recover*
- *25% Improved, relatively independent*
- *25% Improved, but require an extensive support network*
- *15% Hospitalization, unimproved*
- *10% Dead (mainly via suicide, accident, or natural /medical causes)*

~ Schizophrenia.com

SCZ patients are 50 times higher risk for suicide. I've seen that first-hand with my daughter. Every single day we fight against Libby's desire to kill herself. When we admitted her yesterday, she said her plan was to cut her own throat with a knife or stab herself to death. We have the knives and sharp objects locked up, so I'm not sure how she'd accomplish that, and I don't want to ever find out. Heaven help me if she learns how to hang herself.

Libby has a lot of reasons she wants to die, so we try to give her every possible reason to live. The average person with schizophrenia is more of a risk to themselves than others, unless they are of the paranoid subset. Those individuals can be violent, and can be dangerous in psychosis, although not always. Everyone with SCZ is different.

One of the easiest ways to avoid developing SCZ is to avoid brain altering drugs that induce hallucinations like ecstasy, methamphetamines, phencyclamine (PCP), or marijuana. If someone is biologically or genetically predisposed to SCZ, drugs can trigger it from its dormancy. This is called drug-induced schizophrenia. Those who have drug induced SCZ are the ones most likely to recover fully, as opposed to those with biologically related SCZ. Some with milder symptoms are likely to recover with early intervention and proper treatment.

> *Approximately one in 40,000 children will have symptoms of SCZ during the ages of 6-12. In terms of worldwide population, that's .000025% of the population or around 175,000 kids worldwide. ~NMIH*

That's an extremely low number. It is extraordinarily rare for symptoms of SCZ to be recognized before that - I've only ever heard of one other case, and she was 11. Libby started showing signs at two, we just didn't know it until nine years later.

Here's a link to information about another child who suffers from early onset schizophrenia:

https://abcnews.go.com/Health/born-schizophrenic-mentally-ill-children-threaten

For a child, the world becomes a very strange and confusing place with SCZ. Nightmarish visions, an inability to know what's real and what's not, and uncertainty over who to trust can lead to some really awful outcomes. It's not that it's not equally bad for an adult, but in my daughter, there's confusion after Libby comes out of an episode of psychosis. We've had times when she didn't even know who we were because of regression, disorganized thinking, and the cognitive loss from being in extended psychosis.

Worse than that, many clinicians are unable or unwilling to recognize early onset schizophrenia in children. This delayed treatment leads to worse outcomes, longer term suffering, and possibly later in life, an ingrained distrust of the medical community. I already see that for my Libby as she tests each provider. Her question is, "can I be normal?"

If the person answers wrong, Libby will never trust them, because I and her core team have worked with her so extensively. A lot of times they will say, "of course you'll be normal" and I want to smack them. Fail.

Some will take the approach of everyone's "normal" is unique (correct answer). Some say children will outgrow symptoms of psychosis or schizophrenia and their brains are still developing (wrong). Some say the symptoms are due to an overactive imagination the child just needs to control (wrong again). Because of her therapist's work, and ours, Libby is very confident in what's true about her condition. She doesn't waver much, but conflicting responses make her suspicious. I can always tell who has had actual exposure to SCZ, and who hasn't, based on those answers.

Probably the main reason it's so hard to diagnose and treat Libby is because she's a child. Medical providers NEVER listen to her, never trust her, never believe her. When the child has a mental illness, that's understandable. The problem is, they never listen to me either. I've talked until I'm blue in the face about her symptoms not being bipolar, but I must defend against that diagnosis every single time. I've been labeled a hysterical provider by one medical ER professional (my child is catatonic and you're not doing anything, you're damn right I'm hysterical!). I've been accused of coaching my child into her symptoms. I have had CPS called for both neglect and medical neglect for hallucinations. This despite the face she's actively in treatment (this happened this summer).

We have few allies, and few people who care, in the medical field. This makes everything even harder to deal with, because they would take faster action on an adult. Because Liberty's a minor and her brain is still developing, they take a wait and see approach which leads to tremendous suffering. She has said many a time, "Why don't they help me? Why won't anyone just help us?"

December 18, 2018

THE FOUNDATION

I made a decision between yesterday and today. I finally know how to channel all of this into advocacy. I want to formalize some of my planning. I've decided to create a trust and foundation for Libby's cause. I realized there are about 175,000 kids and their families around the world struggling like we are, maybe more.

Because it's such a small population, there's not a lot of resources. Information is hard to come by. I am going to write a book and divide it into two sections - *Part I: Entering the Maze* will be our personal story, our journey, my journals about it, and I will work with Libby to have her share her perspective. I will divide the book up into posts that label each of our perspectives, so it's clear to the reader. *Then Part II: Navigating the Maze* will be educational and advice - information and resources about what I've learned about mental illness, mental health, and the various governmental, educational, and medical resources.

There are an estimated 175,000 kids with SCZ who will grow up to be adults with SCZ. Early intervention will mean a more successful transition to adulthood, and the potential for a better future with SCZ. We may not be able to cure it, but we can make it better.

December 18, 2018

FINDING THE TIME TO WRITE

It's not easy, for sure. If you can believe it, my family helps me find time to write, even my kids. Part of it is I've written two children's books, and both kids love those stories, so they get what my writing means in a real sense. They both love telling people I write books, and then telling them all about how great the books are. My daughter even asked me to make up business cards with the information about the books on them, so she could give them out to people she meets.

On top of that, they know when I finish writing a story, and I'm ready, it's story time. Even at 11 & 13, they love for me to read to them. I guess because as an author I do public readings, it just never occurred to me to stop reading to them. They're oftentimes my first audience. I will cuddle up in bed with them one on one, at separate times, and read the story aloud.

Afterward, we'll talk about it. They give me feedback about what they liked, what they didn't like, and what they would do differently in the story if they wrote it. I make notes, and if I agree with what they say, I incorporate it into the story and then show them I did. It's the best quality time I could ever imagine spending with my kids, and they adore it. I do too. They're always asking me, "mom, when's your next story going to be done?" If I tell them I'm editing it or whatever, they'll say, "well, go finish it! I want to hear it." They are both anxiously awaiting my fantasy novella.

My husband is a big part of it too - Robert pushes me to write, helps me carve out time, and then listens to me vent, gripe, and whine when it's not going well or I'm stuck. Then he patiently helps me work through it. He's also a beta reader and editor for me, plus my brainstorming partner.

We've talked about this as a family. Every single one of them has told me, when I've felt guilty about my writing time, that I do so much for everyone, and I deserve this time. It's as much their gift to me as it is my gift to them. They see how it energizes me, refreshes me, and puts a "sparkle" in my eye (their words, not mine). It benefits them too - both kids have been accused of having a vocabulary too advanced for their peers by the schools (like that's a bad thing, come on!). Unfortunately, Libby lost about 50-70% of her vocabulary this summer, due to severe psychosis, and we're working once again to rebuild it all.

I couldn't imagine not including my family in my writing. I suppose if they weren't interested, it would be different. It's just one of the many family businesses. I know I'm setting an example for my kids and being a strong female role model is important to me. Phoenix needs to see it and Libby does too. Both kids have told me over the years they want to be like me, so I try to impart to them all I know. But I always tell them to be themselves, there can only be one of me!

This is the same with my real estate business. Both kids have expressed an interest in learning more about it, so as they get older, I show them more and more. Both of them have gone to house showings with me (although not participated), especially Libby-whom we can't ever leave alone. When Robert was working as a truck driver, we would show the kids around his rig, and often talked about his work at dinner.

I guess in life one just finds ways to make it work. Sometimes one has to get creative. Sometimes one has to ask for help. One works out ways. My husband mostly takes care of the kids and the house, so that leaves me a lot of time for writing, especially if I'm not working. Currently I'm not working, so I sleep until 8 and am up until midnight. These last few weeks I've lost count of how many thousands of words I've written. On my new nonfiction book, I've written over 5,000 words today alone.

There are times, though, when I can't write. There are times when my plate is overfull, or my brain is overtaxed, when life forces me to look away from my writing and do something else. Right now, both kids are in the hospital. Robert is sick and sleeping a lot. We're a week away from Christmas, so real estate is dead. For now, I'm writing every single minute of the day. It's keeping me sane. It's keeping me from focusing on things I can't do anything about right now - like finances and my kids. It's keeping me optimistic and happy. Being busy is the best way to be for me.

December 18, 2018

A NEW DREAM

I realized last night, based on some estimates from NIMH, it will cost over $7.2 million for Libby's care if she lives to be 80. While Robert and I are supporting her now, and will as long as we are alive, we won't live forever. It's unlikely she will be one of the ones who fully recovers from SCZ (although I would love that, and a lot can change. Maybe they'll find a cure!).

I am writing a book about our journey. All the proceeds will go toward her care, now and in the future. I will form a trust for the funds. The funds that aren't used for Libby can be used for grants for other struggling families with children with a major depressive disorder, SCZ, or schizoaffective disorders. It will be used to change mental health in Texas. Let's change the world for kids with SCZ. Let's make it better for Libby.

December 19, 2018

DOING WHATEVER IT TAKES

I received a call from Libby's treatment facility today. Robert was giving me a nice relaxing massage, because I've been in a lot of pain lately. It must be due to all the long hours typing and researching for my new book, I guess. I was in a good mood and quite unprepared for what was to come.

"I'm calling to let you know the treatment team met regarding Libby, and we don't believe there's anything more we can do for her here. She's being discharged tomorrow, and you have until midnight to pick her up."

I was too stunned to even speak. I tried to ask some questions, to which I was told, try another facility, that Libby's doing fine, and hasn't had a hallucination since she was admitted. By this point, I was in disbelief. All I could think was, "they're kicking my child out and refusing to treat her." Why? These places are there to make money, right? More importantly, they're there to help, right?!

The counselor told me since Libby had already been there for eight weeks, there was no further need for treatment.

This isn't the first time this facility has done something like this. Previously, they lied and said they were discharging Libby due to insurance issues, but this was something else entirely. I attempted to reach the director, the patient advocate, anyone to discuss this. I had to leave voice mail messages for all. Then I called her Medicaid case worker, who called the Medicaid waiver coordinator. Then I called her MHMR case worker and her outpatient therapist. Every single one of them were baffled and astonished.

For the rest of the day and night, my mind has been like an engine being red-lined. For the life of me, I can't figure out why. Why would they do this? Why would they abandon an 11-year-old child this way? What did I say or do wrong? As I questioned everything, analyzed every part of it, I realized I did nothing any different than I had the prior two admissions. I was clear and transparent, honest and detailed, and so was Libby. Yet here we were, adrift in uncertainty.

I sent a letter to Libby's residential therapist and demanded a meeting with the director of the program or higher. I was not going to take this lying down. No one was going to just disregard my child like that. I called Libby and talked to her about her symptoms. She told me she'd hallucinated as recently as the day before. I realized then I couldn't make them treat her. I could stomp my feet, be as ugly and nasty as I wanted to be, and it would do no good. If they were unwilling to treat her while she was symptomatic, nothing I did was going to change that. We are on our own.

Earlier in the day, I'd put my car in the shop for a recall issue. Thankfully, they would be giving me a loaner car to use for a few days. I considered going to San Antonio, but knew I wasn't in any emotional shape to deal with this yet. I also realized if this was the best the treatment center could do, then it was on us to make up the difference. None of their coping skills were working for Libby.

I decided we would start working to create our own coping skills. We'd start working on them when Libby wasn't hallucinating, so she could be well-practiced and strong in them when the hallucinations came. I would teach everyone in the family how to use them, how to support and guide her. That way no matter who was with her, no matter where she was, she could have easy access to support and reminders. I would work with the skills trainer as well. Together, we would create a plan that worked for Libby, whatever it might look like.

Robert and I had a discussion tonight about the books I'm working on writing and how I wanted to interview medical providers. He happened to mention, "Why don't you go back to school and get a master's degree in psychology? That would give you a lot of credibility on the subject. Heck, with all your research and knowledge, you're halfway there anyway." The idea immediately appealed to me. I looked into several programs and learned I didn't need to have an undergraduate degree on the subject. My English degree would easily transfer, giving me two different subjects of expertise. I could even do a minor if I wanted.

That became the plan almost overnight. I will get educated in psychology in order to do the most good for our family and others. I have no desire to be a counselor, but if it will allow me to help our family better, I'll do whatever it takes. Now we have our new plan for the future. I'll start working again to get us financially stable, buy the RV and get moved, then Robert will study to take the test for real estate inspection. Once he's stable with that and we have a six-month reserve again, I'll leave the job to do school, real estate, and manage kids full time. For the first time in two years, we have a plan and dreams again. We have hope. Best of all, we gave it to ourselves. No matter where this journey takes us, we will get through it together.

December 20, 2018

ONE YEAR ANNIVERSARY

I can't believe an entire year has come and gone. At times it seemed to move slow, and others so fast. Where are we after a year? There have been some improvements. We've gotten better at managing Libby's condition. We recognize and understand it better than we ever have. The treatment hasn't stopped the disorder's progression, but it seems to have slowed it down some. It still feels most days like we're treading water instead of moving forward but we're always looking for ways to change that. We have a structure in place.

Financially things are a mess, and I'm praying we come through it. We've been on the edge of a financial cliff for the last few months, and not much more would knock us off. All of us have sought treatment for depression, suicidal thoughts, and anxiety. Each of us have sought help with our issues and tried to help each other through each crisis.

I still grieve most days, but I've come to accept this is the way of things now. It no longer bothers me on the mornings when I wake up and cry in the shower, in the middle of the day, or at night when I go to bed. I've learned to be okay with my tears. I've learned to be okay with the sadness, the fear, the uncertainty, and the soul wrenching pain. I don't let any of it stop me or be a barrier. I've got stuff to do.

Libby has good days and bad days, but she too is learning acceptance. She still grieves, but it's not as often as it was. She knows without a doubt she is loved. When providers ask who her support is, the first word out of her mouth is "my mom and dad." That lifts me. Our relationship is stronger than ever. We've weathered the worst of the storm, we can get through anything now. I hope I never have to test that idea. Puberty isn't that far away, and her diagnosis becomes a whole other animal.

Robert kept his promise that if he ever thought he would kill himself, he would tell me first. Phoenix did too. We were able to get them both help, and they're doing better. Their treatment continues, and likely will for a while.

I was able to get two and a half months of therapy, which pulled me back from a dark, awful place. I realized something about myself: I'm glad that life has given me the inner strength and resilience it has. I need it, every day. There are things required of me now I never could have fathomed.

After one year, I can say I think we're going to be okay, somehow, some way. Sometimes I don't know how we'll get through it, but we always do. We're all together, we're a team, and we're not giving up. We refuse to fail, no matter what. Tomorrow's my 39th birthday and Libby will be home with us, which is the best present I could ever ask for.

Now, we've told our story to the world. We've shined a light into the darkness. We've shared the pain, the heartaches, the joy, and the amazing miracle that is Libby's story. She makes us better, each one of us. Every day we get a little stronger, a little wiser. We learn and we grow. We lift her a little higher, and watch as she lifts herself higher still, with our help. She may not fit into everyone else's idea of "normal," but to us, that's okay. We love her just the same, maybe a little more.

Our tomorrows look brighter. We're dreaming again. We're making plans and working toward goals. We're living life. Schizophrenia isn't getting us down. It knocked us flat for a while. We've had setback after setback. We keep getting back up and living again in a new, better way each time. We know life is but a blink in time. If you're not careful, you might miss it.

NAVIGATING
THE BEHAVIORAL
MAZE

STARTING FROM ZERO

We've come a long way in the past year in our understanding Libby's mental illness. But before that? It was a war zone of our own creation and we didn't even know it. Once we understood more about what Libby was going through, once we understood what psychosis was and its many symptoms, I realized we needed to start over from zero. I took everything I thought I knew about parenting and threw it right out the proverbial window. And I mean everything. I found some resources on-line that talked about having a trust-based relationship with your child and that's where we started. And we started with ourselves.

My husband and I agreed that from that point forward there would be no more losing our tempers, no more screaming. For over a year, when she would scream at us, we'd scream over her in an effort to regain control. If you can imagine, that was a recommended strategy at the time. It went out the window. No more screaming. No corporal punishment under any circumstances, for any reason. We agreed that if one of us felt like he or she would lose their temper, that person would walk away and the other would step in.

We would treat our children with respect and as we would another adult. We would expect them to respond in a similar fashion (although not immediately). And it didn't take long, once we started calming down and communicating with her directly, she started responding. Maybe it's because she's so young. Maybe it's because she was surprised by it. Maybe it's because of who she is. Or perhaps it's a little of all three. Whatever the reason, when we started talking to her like a human being and then listening, she opened up in the most amazing ways. And that's when real understanding began. That's when we started getting in control of our home and our lives again.

The first time she told us about a hallucination, it was everything I could do not to cry. I didn't even know what it was, just that she was seeing something that none of us could. I threw out my skepticism and disbelief. I threw out any suspicion that she could be faking it. I trusted she was telling the truth. And that she needed my help. I accepted all of her feelings of loneliness, fear, sadness. She didn't know what to do with all these things that were happening to her and for years, we'd ignored what was happening to her which left her feeling even more isolated and alone.

Eventually, I did go into the bathroom and wept like a child for five minutes. I wept for the pain in her eyes and the fear in my heart. I wept at the unknown. Then I wiped my tears, tightened down my emotions into a safe place, washed my face with cold water, and went back to her. I'm not sure how but I knew instinctively she would take her emotional cues from me. I did my best to stay cool and calm for her sake. That didn't mean there weren't times I lost it in front of her. Thankfully many of those times were when she was so deep in psychosis, she doesn't remember it.

If your relationship with your child is full of conflict, and you don't know why, I recommend starting over. It means as a parent, you must forgive her for everything she's done in the past. No more bringing up past events. Every single thing. And mean it. The easiest way to do that is to recognize your child is sick. Just like you wouldn't blame a child for feeling bad when they have a cold, you cannot be mad at her for the things she did when in a psychosis.

On top of that, you must do a serious analysis of your own history with the situation. You need to accept the mistakes you've made and forgive yourself for them. It was far easier for me to forgive my child; she didn't know any better. Forgiving myself? I'm still working on that, but I've come a long way. Once you've accepted and forgiven your mistakes comes the even harder part. Then, you have to talk to them about it. You need to identify them to your child, apologize, and ask for their forgiveness. No justifying, no reasons, no excuses. Just a complete, total, heartfelt apology. You might cry and that's okay for them to see if it's genuine. If you need a therapist's help, seek it.

I also researched everything I could get my hands on for six solid months. Every spare moment I had was spent researching and trying to understand. I joined forums and parents groups to read about other parents' experiences. I learned what worked, what didn't, things to do, things to watch out for. There wasn't a lot of information but there was a lot of help and support, which gave me the strength to get through some of the hardest circumstances I've ever experienced. The schizophrenia.com website was by far the most helpful and knowledgeable, but there were several Facebook groups that helped tremendously too. Parents of Kids with Schizophrenia was one such group, just chock full of concerned family members trying to do exactly what I was doing: helping someone with mental illness. I still spend a lot of time researching, seeking new resources, new strategies, new ideas. Science is always changing and I'm hoping one day we'll have more answers than we do now.

Every child is different and unique so what worked for us may or may not work for you. A lot of it is trial and error. I know with my son we've seen less results from the strategies we use with Libby. The main benefit to using the strategies is by doing so, you won't lose your mind or inadvertently cause mental anguish to your child.

TREAT YOUR CHILD WITH RESPECT AS YOU WOULD AN ADULT

If your child has been diagnosed with major depressive disorder, psychosis, schizophrenia or any serious mental illness, they've got a very challenging path ahead of them. Don't make it worse by invalidating their feelings because they'll just do whatever they can to get what they need which is love, acceptance, understanding, and most of all help for their issues. Our children are capable of so much more than we give them credit for and I'm just as guilty of this as any other parent. Every time my child transitioned through a phase it was a challenge for me to keep up. It seemed like she was constantly changing. As soon as I felt like I'd caught up and could take a break, she'd make another milestone or leap another hurdle.

One of my earliest examples of this is potty training. I had gotten pretty used to pull ups and after numerous failures to transition forward, I just gave up. Then one day, out of the blue, she didn't want to do pull ups anymore. I later laughed because just a few days before, I had gotten a huge box of pull ups from Sam's. I ended up gifting them to another parent who had a child still doing pull ups. We'd already opened them and used a few so I couldn't return them.

As she's progressed with this disorder, I've struggled to adjust as she learns and develops new skills. I must be very mindful of those changes. I find praising her for her achievements makes it easier to accept her new skills and advancements. At eleven, almost twelve, she's become a very serious, mature young lady who is very capable of explaining her symptoms and being involved in the process so I do my best to include her despite an instinct to protect her from it. Trying to protect her from the realities of this disorder does nothing but confuse and scare her so we talk openly about it and anything else that comes up.

ACCEPT THE DIAGNOSIS

This is such a hard step, but acceptance is key to communicating. If you child feels you don't believe her, she won't come to you honestly and tell you what's going on. And unlike with a physical injury, you need your child to confide in you so you can help. With mental illness comes a lot of different kinds of symptoms. Some are physical and visible, like flat affect. Others, like the desire to die are invisible symptoms. If your child doesn't share these symptoms, you'll never know they're there. You accepting the diagnosis, believing in it, gives your child the freedom to do so as well. Which is so important to the treatment and healing process. The sooner there's acceptance, the sooner that complex process can start.

STRESS HOW IMPORTANT HONESTY IS

It's very important to have a conversation about honesty, not only with you but with providers. Children need to learn how to do this as the instinct is to hide what's wrong. Feelings of shame, fear, and anger are all normal. Asking for help is always hard, no matter how old you are.

TELL HER YOU LOVE HER NO MATTER WHAT

A mentally ill child is more vulnerable than one who's not mentally ill, so reassuring her regularly you love and accept her is important to building up her self-esteem and confidence. It's also critical to keeping the communication channels open. All your child wants to know is that if she tells you these terrible things, you'll accept them, and still love her no matter what. Confessing some of these feelings can be a very vulnerable, intimate thing to do for your child because they want your love more than anything. I regularly tell my daughter, "I love you forever and always, no matter what." I especially do this when she's symptomatic, in a treatment facility or recently released. It always makes her smile and it's a reminder that no matter what happens I will be there for her.

TELL HER YOU'RE PROUD OF HER

Asking for help is hard for anyone. But children have an especially difficult time because they haven't even had a chance to learn how to do that. It's up to you as the parent to guide her in this process and teach her how. And then to reward her when she does it by telling her you're proud of her for taking care of herself and getting help. Learning to be an advocate for yourself is a long process but she'll pick up cues from you as you go through the process.

EXTRA TIME TOGETHER

I spend extra time with my daughter doing non-medical related stuff together once a week. Oftentimes we're so busy with appointments, it can get lost in the shuffle that we're not spending time together. We'll cuddle in bed, I'll read her a story, we'll watch a movie, go on a drive or to a restaurant, or we'll just be in the same room together. Being comfortable with each other makes it easier to communicate with each other when there's a problem. This is an excellent way to achieve that.

One of the hardest part of having a child with mental illness is being their advocate. You are the only defense in a complex situation they do not have the skills to navigate on their own. At the same time, you're trying to get care for your child, you're always defending them, sharing the relevant history, detailing the problems being experienced, and helping your child express properly what's going on. You're standing up for them and making sure they receive the best possible care. You're also busy trying to find answers to countless questions.

Early in the process I learned that my emotions would get in the way of the whole process. If I lashed out at providers, they would shut down. The person who suffered from that wasn't me. It was my child. Because they then wouldn't be as effective at treating her needs. So I learned to ask a lot of questions and control my reaction to things. By no means was this perfect. There were many a time where I would cry detailing aspects of her history or the current crisis but for the most part, I controlled my emotions to communicate better.

Being an advocate for a child with mental illness is an exhausting, frustrating, and maddening process at times. It will require skills you never knew you had or needed. It requires always asking the question, "Why?" It means asking, "What do you do next?" It means being an active participant. No one knows your child like you so get involved and be part of the solution.

Being an advocate is also one of the most rewarding experiences you'll have in this process. Watching your child progress and learn new skills will have you in awe. It can feel like a miracle when they master a new skill.

People who talk to Libby when she's medicated and lucid are always so impressed by her intelligence. That makes me laugh and shake my head at the ignorance. Of course, she's smart! Schizophrenia is a terrible disorder, but schizophrenics are commonly highly intelligent people who are struggling with an illness. If you can manage the illness, it's possible to have a certain level of function. How much is different for each person.

This year Libby stopped feeling like and acting like a victim. She now wears her diagnosis like a badge of honor. She has accepted her desire to commit suicide and hasn't given into it. She loves helping others, especially when she's in the facility. And I've never been prouder of her for that. Our advocating for her gave her the courage and strength to get help. The rest she did on her own. And that's what advocacy does. It allows your child to be open to getting help.

***

Suicide is one of the most preventable cause of death in the world and is the 10th leading cause of death worldwide. Men are four times more likely than women and a large reason for suicide is mental illness. Adults with schizophrenia are 50% more likely to commit suicide than people with other illnesses. I have seen this myself with Libby, who has been suicidal since the age of seven. There's is nothing scarier than knowing within your child, every single day, is a desire to die. You can never fully let your guard down. But there are many things you can do and we've come up with a number of strategies to help her and us, cope with this issue.

THE PROMISE

When my daughter was old enough, around nine, we made a promise to each other. She promised to me that she would come to me before hurting herself and I promised to stop anything I was doing to help her. She has kept that promise over the years, despite having a plan.

REMOVE ACCESS

This one is tough and a bit inconvenient, but you have to do everything you can to remove access to things that could be used. We lock up all the knives in the house. Many of her plans involved slitting her throat or stabbing herself. While it may seem unrealistic, we must take the possibility seriously. We bought a combo lock that only her father and I know the combo for and locked up a drawer of our knives and scissors. Even the kid friendly scissors.

We have also locked up our gun in a safe in our closet and put a combo on it that only we know. We have put a lock on our bedroom door to prevent access to medications that could be used for overdosing. This doesn't prevent every possibility because she could still attempt to hang herself but that would be very hard for her to do. She's also monitored by us around 20 hours a day. There's a slight window between midnight and 4 a.m. or 2 a.m. to 6 a.m. when we're both asleep but we try to stagger our schedules to increase monitoring and reduce the chances of her harming herself. So far, for the last five years, these measures have prevented her harming herself.

BEING OPEN

I have opened myself up to my daughter and shared with her my own story about suicide. A parent's natural instinct is to protect your child from dark topics but sharing this with her actually helped her. It made her see she wasn't alone, and that I understand what she's dealing with. We've had many discussions about ways to cope with the feeling and I've let her know that regularly I will have these thoughts. I think of a promise I made myself to an officer years ago. I think about her and what hurting myself would do to her. I think about my husband and what leaving him alone would mean. I think about the people it would hurt and it automatically pulls me back from the brink. Because I would never do anything to hurt them. We remind her she can always come talk to us about her feelings, especially if she feels like she wants to die.

I simply let her talk and listen carefully. I tell her I'm so sorry she feels that way, remind her of her promise and how much I love her, how important she is. Then we try to find a solution together. I will ask her if there's anything I can do to help her feel better. Sometimes she just needs extra hugs and cuddles to make her feel better. Sometimes she needs to go do something fun. Sometimes nothing seems to work and so we go to therapy. If her risk is high, we admit her. **The number one thing we don't do are ignore it.** We are serious and mindful of this every single time because when she feels this way, she needs help to feel better. Many times, because of her age, she cannot figure out how to fix it herself. As she's gotten older, she's gotten better in this area but it's still tough for her. And even when she's an adult, we will continue to take it seriously because we want her to come to us for help. We never want to undermine the trust she's put in us on this. It's too important. Because it could mean the difference between life and death.

THERAPY

We've done some very intensive therapy over the years to address this issue, both inpatient and outpatient. And we constantly reinforce the message that she is loved, she is special, she is precious, and we do not want to lose her. Ever. In this world, so many people feel unloved, unappreciated, unsupported, and when life gets hard, it becomes this horrible feeling like life isn't worth living. I know, I've been there myself. Many times. So we do everything we can do support her in this way, both verbally and through our actions.

THE REALITY

None of this means I don't have nightmares of her killing herself. I've dreamed multiple times of finding her in our kitchen sitting against the stove with her wrists cut and blood everywhere. I dreamed of her being hit by a car. I've dreamed of her drowning in the bathtub or a neighbor's pool. I've dreamed of finding her dead countless times.

As a mother, that's my living nightmare and one of my biggest terrors. They are some of the worst dreams I've ever had in my life and they haunt me vividly every day. But while that lives within me, I have compartmentalized it and you will need to as well. You cannot let the idea of losing your child consume you. Because it can eat you alive and take you to a place so dark you'll fear you will never see the light again.

I have accepted that I may do everything humanly possible and one day it may not be enough. Where there's a will there's a way. Paranoid schizophrenia is a horrible mental illness that twists its victims in terrible ways every day. It's a constant battle to protect her from herself and lift her up as high as we can so that when those horrible times come, she hopefully has the resiliency to withstand the onslaught. Or to ask for help when it gets to be too much.

DISCIPLINE STRATEGIES

Every child is unique so there's never going to be a strategy that works with every child. We see that in our household in the ways that each of our children respond to us. However, there are a couple of hard and fast rules we've come to follow and live by to help promote health in our children.

NO CORPORAL PUNISHMENT

I've been a victim of abuse and I understand clearly the difference between abuse and corporal punishment. However, think for a moment of yourself as an adult. You're at work and you've made a mistake that's going to cost the company money. What if your boss' solution was to spank you? What if he made you pull your pants down in front of your co-workers then spanked you? How would you feel? Would you feel embarrassed? Afraid? Angry? Would you care why you were spanked, or would you be so emotionally overwhelmed from the experience that the reasoning became lost to you? Would you forget why you were spanked entirely? I've never believed in disciplining children this way and have a great deal of respect for that fact that they are miniature versions of us.

We have tried in the past, against my better judgment, using spanking as a punishment. I could ask either child why they were spanked and, in the moment, they could tell me verbatim. They were simply parroting back to me what I'd said. Ask them 24 hours later and they would be unable to recollect why, they just knew they'd been spanked, and it hurt. A year later, all they knew still was to be afraid of a spanking. Sure, the behavior improved temporarily but not long term. The lesson was gone and never truly learned or retained.

For a mentally ill child especially, corporal punishment does more harm than good. Even for the short duration in which we employed this tactic, both of our children became withdrawn and afraid of us. In addition, they became afraid to ever make a mistake and terrified of doing something wrong. They became afraid to come to us.

It created enormous fear, anxiety, and stress that was counterproductive to their mental health. And we weren't even using it that often! Regardless of whether you believe me, or you believe corporal punishment works, think about how you would want to be treated. Would it be with love, kindness, and respect, or a heavy hand? Would you want someone to teach you in a loving kind manner, or punish you for doing wrong? Would you like it if someone screamed at you for doing something wrong? We've all lost it at some point or another. The point is from now on to train yourself to take a deep breath and find another way. Walk away if you need to and come back when you're calmer.

In our household, I made a rule with my husband. Absolutely, positively, no corporal punishment for any reason. No exceptions. There is nothing our children can do to earn that as a punishment. Nothing. And I've had to enforce that boundary with my husband.

You'll have to stand firm and ready to intervene if your spouse or partner decides corporal punishment is the best route to use.

While it's never good for parents to be on different pages, this is one area where it's okay to differ and protect your child(ren). It's important to talk about this in advance privately so your spouse isn't caught off guard. I've spent a lot of time mediating and intervening to help work out conflicts in our house, especially with our son who seems in recent years to have a mind of his own and to disregard the rules.

ESTABLISH A ROUTINE

Children thrive with a routine. It can be as rigid as you feel is necessary. This teaches them to self-regulate and follow a schedule, which is an important life skill. It takes **years** for kids to learn this, so don't let it frustrate you if they don't catch on immediately. Consistency is key. You're showing them to respect boundaries and rules, which takes time. Kids are all about having fun. But following the rules takes hard work. Some ways we've done this is we try to get up at the same time each day, even weekends. Part of this is due to medications which need to be given around the same time each day. My husband is not really great about this but I'm often up by 8:30, regardless of what time I went to sleep.

MAKE EXPECTATIONS CLEAR

Both of our children have clear expectations. For our daughter, it's try her best every day, take meds, do her hygiene, spend time doing schoolwork every day except Sunday, have respect for others, and follow the rules. For our son, it's a little different because he's not dealing with as many issues. For him it's follow the rules and have respect, do his personal hygiene every day, do school work from 8 until 5 each day, do his chores correctly, and not abuse his sister. We put a lot of emphasis on respect - toward others and toward yourself. My husband and I model that in our relationship with each other and we show them all the time ways to be respectful toward each other. We try to teach them how to have empathy and teach them what the various disorders mean and look like.

COMMON PROBLEMS

It's time for open enrollment! If you're fortunate enough to have a group policy, great! Or perhaps you're using the Healthcare Marketplace. No matter what your options might be, take care because the choices you make now will be with you for the next year or until the next open enrollment, whichever comes first. Choosing a bad plan can be devastating for your finances, especially if you have a mentally ill child.

At some point, you may need to investigate alternative health insurance sources like Medicaid if symptoms are severe and difficult to manage. But know that providers prefer private insurance over that of Medicaid because they pay better and are easier to work with. Private insurance companies also often have better networks. The double-edged sword is you will do battle with the insurance company to authorize care, so it's just as important to choose the company wisely. You can also stack insurance policies by having a private insurance and a Medicaid plan to allow for less out of pocket expense.

If you have time, it can be good to call and ask questions or look for answers in the plan documents.

WHAT'S THE LIMIT FOR MENTAL HEALTH TREATMENT? IS THERE A LIFETIME CAP?

Some plans will limit the number of days, number of stays, total dollar amount spent in a calendar year, lifetime maximum, and more. Some plans don't cover mental health services at all! Know this part of the plan well before you choose. Obamacare also known as the Affordable Care Act (ACA) did make substantial strides in the individual and family markets for ensuring coverage of mental health issues by requiring coverage be offered as part of the plan. But that comes with a price tag as insurers can increase premiums. Large group plans are not required to offer these benefits.

WHAT'S THE OUT OF POCKET MAXIMUM?

This is the maximum amount you will have to pay out of pocket in a plan year. If you have a bad mental health year, it can happen. I was very surprised to find our out of pocket maximum could be met in less than three weeks when my daughter was admitted to two different facilities in one month at the beginning of 2018. For over nine months, medical staff were astonished when I told them the out of pocket maximum for our plan was met. Oftentimes they didn't believe me and when it was verified their demeanor turned from suspicion to sympathy.

DO THEY HAVE 24/7 SUPPORT?

Sometimes you may need to talk to Member Services at 3 a.m. because of a crisis. Or if you work full time, being able to call after traditional business hours means you don't have to give up your lunch break to get things done. Having 24/7 support or even just longer support hours for members can make a huge difference.

A NURSE'S HOTLINE?

This can be an invaluable resource if it's available, for asking questions quickly of someone experienced rather than your Facebook group.

ANY EXTRAS?

Some insurance companies are starting to include some nice bonuses to subscribers, especially for children, like gift cards for well checkups and toys for doing certain necessary annual tasks.

My commercial insurance company, Blue Cross Blue Shield, assigned a licensed social worker to follow up with us regarding my daughter's care. This was an invaluable resource and great source of support throughout Libby's treatment. So much so, that I chose BCBS for her Medicaid provider, knowing we would be assigned a staff member as a resource. The case manager would call quarterly to check up on her progress, or if she had been hospitalized, would call for more information. It was an invaluable conduit for making sure the insurance company was on the same page with us in regard to authorizing her treatment. On the Medicaid side, this individual has been a huge support both emotionally and logistically as I worked to get my daughter treatment. Treat these folks like the allies they are!

WHEN INSURANCE DENIES

First, don't panic! I made this mistake and it just made everything worse. Hearing the words, "The insurance company denied more days of treatment" will send a chill and terror through your heart, especially if you know your child isn't doing well. The words, "We're not sure if insurance will approve more days" will do the same because they could lead to a denial. But there's options for you.

The Health Insurance Portability and Accountability Act (HIPAA) is a very necessary but oftentimes confusing and frustrating privacy law governing who can have access to private medical records. What this means for you as a parent is peace of mind that your child's mental health information won't get into the wrong hands, but also a lot of documentation. You'll need to provide access to every medical provider who needs it through a release called a medical authorization. Typically, these expire in a year unless you extend it longer.

It's important to be organized and keep an easy to access list of previous and current medical providers handy. I keep mine in a Google Sheet so that I can keep it updated easily, access it from almost anywhere, and print from anywhere that I have access to a printer. I usually keep a printed copy with me because most mental health facilities won't let you keep your phone with you beyond the front lobby for privacy reasons.

In the sheet I include the name, address, fax number, contact names and titles, and email addresses if I have them. I can access it easily from my smart phone for locations that allow me to have my phone like doctors' offices and therapists.

It's important to study initially the documentation you're given and to know your rights as a parent. The Department of Health & Human Services also provides online access to the rules. You can access it at: https://www.hhs.gov/hipaa/for-individuals/index.html

Providing access to the various medical records from your child's previous and ongoing care is paramount to successful treatment and ensures the staff treating your child handle her appropriately. Oftentimes though, you can't easily get access to records yourself in a timely enough fashion. This seems counter-intuitive but it's easier for medical providers to communicate directly as opposed to a parent or caregiver and risk misinformation. Any time I meet with a new provider, I let them know I will need to provide them with records releases so they can request records of her prior treatment. At this point, there are reams and reams of documentation, far more than I can keep up with. I do keep up with her latest diagnosis every time she's discharged, and if it changes, I question it.

There's a very helpful section about parents of children with mental illness at:

https://www.hhs.gov/sites/default/files/when-your-child.pdf

COMMON PROCEDURES AND TESTS

- MRI
- Lab work
- Neuro-psychology testing
- Well visits
- Psychiatric Evaluations

NAVIGATING THE FINANCIAL MAZE

Having a child with mental illness is a financial challenge. Between deductibles, copays, coinsurance, plus all the unseen costs of time, travel costs, food, and the emotional cost, it's an expensive endeavor even if the child's symptoms aren't severe.

Some households, like ours, have multiple children with mental illness or mental health issues. Our son is high functioning autistic with ADHD and PTSD. While he's not as severe as our daughter, his needs are no less important than hers, they're just different.

Both are expensive and on any given day, can stretch anyone thin mentally and emotionally. Not to mention the budget. Unless you're a triple digit gross income, it's a challenge to juggle the expenses. NMIH estimates it costs as much as $60,000 a year to treat someone with a serious mental illness.

BUDGETING FOR ROUTINE CARE

There will be regular costs for treating your child's mental illness. If you bank allows it, I would set up a separate account with its own bank account. If you have an employer who offers an HSA or

FSA plan, great! Use it! Contribute the maximum. I have exceeded mine every single year for almost 10 years.

Formula to use: Copay x total number of visits = annual cost

PHYSICIAN OFFICE SICK VISITS

Children get sick, that's a given. I have been fortunate my daughter is physically exceptionally healthy. The worst she typically gets is a head cold or stomach bug. In 2017, I caught two different types of flu (thanks to my son). My daughter never got sick. I'm typically the same way, I don't get sick often, but when I do, I'm very sick and need medical care. Know your child's history. If you have an HSA and can afford it, budget on the high side. I usually do two sick visits a year for each of my kids. If the copay is $30 each, that's $120.00 for the year.

PSYCHIATRIST OFFICE VISITS

Based on your child's condition, your psychiatrist's preferences, and whether or not there's relapses, the number of times you'll see the psychiatrist can vary. For my daughter, I had one doctor who wanted to see her once a month. Another was every 90 days. If you're not sure, plan for once a month. Depending on the medication and where your child is in their treatment will determine how often they are seen and will change as they progress. You can always use the funds for something else (and there will be something else).

THERAPIST COPAY

This cost can vary as well, depending on where your child is in their treatment. If they're new to treatment, one to two visits a week is common. If they are more stable, then biweekly or monthly may be common. A minimum budget would be monthly. For us, we budget two visits a week and if we don't use them, the money budgeted outside of an FSA or HSA rolls over to the next year in our savings account.

SPECIALIST COPAY

This can vary and will depend on the conditions your child has. If there's physical wellness issues like diabetes, or asthma, these will be higher. Use your best judgment and aim to budget high.

PRESCRIPTION DRUGS

I price shop our prescriptions. Oftentimes Walmart or our local grocery store has the best price but Walgreens or CVS often has a better supply and easier access. This one's easy - just budget the monthly amount you spend but know that it may vary if you're still working on finding the right medications. Be sure to include asthma supplies in this if your child has it - a nebulizer if you don't have one, inhalers, and new parts for the nebulizer are usually all needed regularly depending on usage.

OVER THE COUNTER (OTC) MEDICATION AND SUPPLEMENTS

In our house, everyone takes Spring Valley Melatonin at night, even the children. We get the gummy ones because they taste good and act fast. A year's supply at 2018 prices if you take only one a night is about $30 a year. We also keep Tylenol, Advil, Midol, and some multi vitamins in the house. Our OTC budget is about $150.00 a year for a family of four.

URGENT CARE

Kids will be kids, and kids with mental illness are no different. I budget two visits a year per child.

LAB WORK

My daughter typically needs her blood work checked twice or more a year. My son was at one time monthly, but now doesn't need blood work. This may vary from year to year. Unlike prescriptions and office visits, this cost can vary a lot so it pays to shop around for pricing. Typically, the cost will be based on your co-insurance rather than a co-pay.

ACUTE CARE

You should budget, if possible, for a minimum of one visit a year. Chances are good that your child may have a serious mental health crisis as she ages. In particular, the teenage years are especially vulnerable years.

Bonus tip: If possible, simply budget to use your entire out of pocket maximum each year, whatever that may be. If you don't use it, great! But that way you'll have it if you ever need it. Make sure to replenish it each year.

HANDLING

THE EMERGENCY ROOM BILL

At some point, it's likely you'll need to visit an ER with your child. Whether it's for a physical or mental health emergency, the process is exhausting and unpleasant for everyone.

In the ER you'll be asked to fill out and sign several forms, usually a HIPAA form, a consent to treat, and a financial form as authorization to bill your insurance, and if they don't pay, bill you.

A rule of thumb I have for these forms. I never give social security numbers for myself or my child. Doing so allows them to pursue collections and place on your credit report if you don't pay. I refuse to make it any easier for them to do so. They may be able to find a way to get it anyway, but I never volunteer that information. And my child's social is an absolute no. 100% of the time. There's no reason for them to have it. They have her ID number and that's sufficient. I've never had a facility request it after the fact. But it has kept some information from popping onto my credit report over the years.

Many hospitals now will make attempts to collect payment from you at the time of service. It's a terrible, callous practice because you're at your most stressed, exhausted, and overwhelmed.

Making any kind of decision at that stage is not a good idea. I've even had one person say, "So will that be cash, check, or charge for the $3,200 owed today?" I laughed in her face and told her very clearly to get out. Staff may be rude to you and pressure you but stand firm against these tactics. You don't need to be mean, angry, or react to them but you can put a firm boundary and hold to it.

It's important to remember first and foremost, hospitals are estimating your bill. They have no actual idea what your bill will be, so they put in the charges they expect, which may or may not be correct, and then try to get you to pay your estimated portion before billing the insurance. If your bill exceeds your out of pocket maximum, or you have other charges that are submitted first and lower your deductible, you'll never know it. You'll never know you overpaid what is actually owed. They certainly aren't going to audit and refund if you've overpaid them. (Of course, if you have a copay that's reasonable, feel free to pay that but most people have a deductible to meet first).

Furthermore, if a submitted charge is wrong or a code is incorrect, you'll have paid for services that were invalid. A lot of times insurance companies are good at catching these but it's a good idea to review the charges just in case as most review systems are automated.

My standard statement, in a cool and professional manner, is, "Please bill my insurance and then bill me for my portion." If they persist in asking for an amount I can pay that day, I say zero. There's no point arguing with these folks and they truly do not care what your story is. No matter how bad it is for you, they've probably heard worse. And they're completely desensitized to it.

Save your breath, tell them no, and move on. You've got much bigger things to worry about.

WHEN HOSPITAL BILLS ARRIVE

When you receive bills for medical services, it's important to review these carefully. It's tedious and a pain, but it's necessary. I have caught countless errors, including services that weren't even rendered. The insurance company may catch some of the more obvious ones. Typically, they'll catch when services rendered should be bundled but are billed separately instead. I've seen hospitals bill for both medication and the administration of it which should be a bundled service nowadays. There are a lot of opportunities for billing errors and while I don't subscribe to the many conspiracy theories out there, mistakes happen.

In addition, fraud does exist. One provider we used for several years, Little River Healthcare, went out of business suddenly and is being investigated for their billing practices. I fought with them for six months when they billed me for a sick visit that was a well visit and would have cost me $250 (and should have been free). They did that because the well visits don't pay as well due to the negotiated rate. They also attempted to bill us for lab work that wasn't performed to the tune of $16,000. I brought that to the insurance company's attention and the charges were reversed.

There's an online website that allows you to look up CPT codes and other diagnostic codes on a medical bill. Hospitals are required to use specific forms for billing and while they won't provide you those without a specific request, the bills should be pretty specific. In addition, the Explanation of Benefits (EOB) from your health insurance will give you good insights into the charges as well. Review and compare both documents for accuracy to make sure it's correct.

One resource for this is through the Medicare website. They update it annually.

https://www.cms.gov/medicare/coding/hcpcsreleasecodesets/alpha-numeric-hcpcs.html

Here's another one:
https://www.cgsmedicare.com/medicare_dynamic/hcpcs/search.asp

https://www.cms.gov/medicare/coding/nationalcorrectcodinited/nci-edits-physicians-items/cms046391.html

NOTE: You should never have to pay for this as there are free resources available.

USING CREDIT CARDS TO PAY

Do not do this unless you can pay off the balance immediately. Healthcare is expensive enough without adding interest to it. (Debit cards don't count). Here's something I learned after a dental procedure years ago to have my teeth done. Once you turn a medical bill into a credit card bill or loan, the protections in place regarding medical debt vanish. The statute of limitations changes. Your consumer rights change. And if, for whatever reason you can't and don't want to pay, it will affect your credit. Don't use these methods to pay for your health care unless a provider refuses to treat and it's not a crisis. Ask about interest free payment plans or payment arrangements.

Another rule of thumb. If the provider has billed you, you can pay any amount. Don't let them pressure you into paying more than you can afford. If they receive an amount from you, even as little as $5, they generally cannot send you to collections. I use my bank bill pay service to send payments each month of an amount I can afford. Even if it takes ten years, this is far better than having a credit card debt that collects interest every month and thus sinks you deeper and deeper in debt. If you've already done this, make a double the minimum payment to help get that debt paid off and reduce the interest paid. For example, if your minimum payment is $40, then pay $80. You'll have it paid off in no time.

DEALING WITH COLLECTIONS

It's bound to happen. Amongst all the chaos that goes along with life in general as well as managing a child with a mental illness, a bill is likely to be missed. Or maybe it just can't be paid. In either case, if it is sent to collections because the medical provider isn't willing to work with me on it, I refuse to pay a dime.

After some time has passed, I will check my credit report and dispute the charges. If at that point, I can afford it I will request to pay for deletion and get the promise in writing. Then I can provide this to the credit bureaus to remove it. There's a lot more that goes into this and there are resources on-line to help. Creditboards.com is an excellent resource for dealing with credit issues. If you have the funds, you can have your credit report professionally disputed but be careful because not all services are created equal.

Finally, if I talk about these things on the phone, I'm very careful about what I say as the calls are often recorded and can restart the statute of limitations. Tread carefully.

ABOUT THE AUTHOR

Charity Marie is a dedicated mother of two special needs children and an award-winning author, Realtor, Certified Paralegal, and entrepreneur. Her passion is changing lives, and she brings that to everything she does.

DON'T MISS IT!

Hope can be found even in the darkest of minds...

CHARITY MARIE

UNDERSTANDING
LiBBY
A MOTHER'S JOURNEY WITH CHILDHOOD PARANOID SCHIZOPHRENIA

Be sure to check out book 2 – 3 of the series, which continues our journey. They are packed full of tips, tricks, advice, and anecdotes about our family's experiences, which have helped shape our approach. These books are the first to give a both a first-hand account as well as a roadmap for success in managing a mentally ill child, by a parent who's been through it. This information is helpful regardless of the illness, but especially for childhood paranoid schizophrenia.

www.ingramcontent.com/pod-product-compliance
Lightning Source LLC
Chambersburg PA
CBHW030247030426
42336CB00009B/292